# Tapping
## for the
# Gifted Child

# Tapping
## for the
# Gifted Child

Using the Emotional Freedom Techniques
To Address the Unique Challenges
of Giftedness

Wendy Chamberlin

Copyright © 2019 by Wendy Chamberlin

Published by Zero K Press
ZeroKPress.com

Cover design: Gina E. Mallonee
Cover photo: Gina E. Mallonee
GinaCreative.com

All rights reserved. No part of this book may be reproduced in whole or in part by any means, mechanical, photographic, or electronic, or by any information storage and retrieval system now known or hereafter invented – other than for "fair use" as brief quotations embodied in articles and reviews – without prior written permission of the publisher.

The material in this book is for informational purposes only and is not intended to substitute for the advice and care of your physician or mental health provider. The author and publisher expressly disclaim responsibility for any adverse effects that may result from the use or application of the information contained in this book.

ISBN 978-0-96-006591-2

eBook ISBN 978-0-96-006592-9

*For Claire, without whom
I would never have learned any of this.*

It is easier to build strong children
than to repair broken men.

- Widely attributed to Frederick Douglass
(Ransom, 2014)

# Contents

Introduction    1

## PART ONE:
### The Emotional Freedom Techniques

| | | |
|---|---|---|
| CHAPTER ONE: | Giftedness and the Emotional Freedom Techniques | 9 |
| CHAPTER TWO: | What to Do and What to Expect | 26 |
| CHAPTER THREE: | Triggering | 48 |

## PART TWO:
### Academic Challenges

| | | |
|---|---|---|
| CHAPTER FOUR: | Boredom | 65 |
| CHAPTER FIVE: | Imposter Syndrome | 74 |
| CHAPTER SIX: | Twice Exceptionality | 87 |

## PART THREE:
### Emotional Challenges

| | | |
|---|---|---|
| CHAPTER SEVEN: | Perfectionism | 103 |
| CHAPTER EIGHT: | Isolation | 125 |
| CHAPTER NINE: | Depression | 143 |
| CHAPTER TEN: | Anxiety | 167 |
| CHAPTER ELEVEN: | Positive Disintegration | 181 |

**PART FOUR:**

**The Apple Doesn't Fall Far from the Tree**

| | | |
|---|---|---|
| CHAPTER TWELVE: | Parental Denial | 193 |
| CHAPTER THIRTEEN: | Parental Triggering | 206 |
| CHAPTER FOURTEEN: | Parental Acceptance | 217 |

Resources   221

Acknowledgements   224

References   226

Index   230

# Introduction

As a rule, I think most of the people who know me would not describe me as a nutcase. I have a good memory and a quick mind. I love research and planning, and I'm a critical thinker who tends not to take things on faith.

I'm also a certified practitioner of the Emotional Freedom Techniques (EFT). I help people to heal their emotions by talking about their feelings while tapping on their faces, which admittedly sounds pretty crazy.

The strange discrepancy between critical thinker and energy healer leads many people to ask me, "How did you come to be involved with EFT, of all things?"

It's a fair question.

My journey began a few years ago, when a friend came up to me quite out of the blue and said, "I think I'm supposed to teach you EFT."

I'd heard about EFT in passing. The Emotional Freedom Techniques is a healing modality that involves tapping on points on the body while talking about troubling issues. It's like talk therapy combined with acupressure, but to be honest, I was none too sure about acupressure, either. The idea that tapping on my face while talking about my problems could cause those problems to dissipate seemed farfetched, to say the least.

So despite her desire to help, I replied, "No, thanks. I'm good."

Within the year, I found myself in a deep depression and began a rigorous round of auto-therapy. I read books, did extensive journaling, meditation, and visualizations, and used self-hypnosis and guided imagery; I even tried art therapy. They all worked, to a point. I was able to understand what had happened in my life, and I could see how the pieces fit together, but I couldn't seem to *feel* better. Cognitive understanding wasn't translating to emotional healing.

Somewhat in desperation, I went back to my friend about a year after our initial conversation and said, "I think you're supposed to teach me EFT."

The very next day, she was kind enough to teach me the basics of EFT, but while I was eager to try this new tool, I didn't feel confident using it. I waited three days while I tried to figure out what to do, and finally decided to try tapping along with a YouTube video, just so I didn't have to figure out what to say on my own.

I selected one at random that seemed to address the issue that had been weighing on my mind. It was a five-minute video, but within about twenty seconds of beginning to work, I was sobbing uncontrollably and continued to do so for nearly 20 minutes. When the tears stopped, I tapped along with the video again and got through it without tears, though I did choke up at a few points. Then I slept a long, hard, dreamless sleep, and the next morning I tried tapping with the video again.

This time, all the emotional charge was gone, and the video was almost boring. I felt entirely differently about the issue, as if a weight had been lifted. Given the astonishing change in my response to those few minutes of video, and the immediate, and ultimately permanent, change in the way I think about that issue, I was wholly convinced that EFT worked, and I've never looked back.

While EFT looks and sounds strange, inexplicable, or even "woo-woo," in my own life it has worked wonders to help me heal emotional pains both old and new. I've found that emotions and memories processed using this tool have been permanently altered. It's not that I lose my memory of painful events, it's just that it no longer hurts to recall them. I've found that EFT has helped me heal.

My own experience with tapping persuaded me to teach a few friends, who also had consistently positive results. Their results encouraged me to learn more about the tool so that I could be more effective in my use of it. Then I shared with more people, until my positive feedback loop finally convinced me to become certified as an EFT practitioner in the hope I could share this instrument as widely as possible.

Thanks to my course of study, I can tell you the theories behind the technique. I can explain concepts like energy flow and polarity reversals, and while I'm not entirely sold on the theoretical underpinnings, neither am I certain that they're wrong. Energy medicine has been used successfully around the globe for over 5,000 years, and the emerging field of energy psychology is building on this foundation with impressive results.

I continue to read the scientific literature on how and why EFT works, exploring areas such as neuroplasticity – the ability of the brain to rewire itself in light of changing conditions; epigenetics – how genes are expressed in the body; and quantum medicine – the application of quantum physics to medical practice, which turns out to be a field that essentially doesn't exist yet. I think there's a great deal about people, energy, and health that we as a species don't yet understand.

Although I'm not convinced that the purveyors of the Emotional Freedom Techniques have all the answers, I *am* convinced that they have developed a tool that works. Over and over again, I've seen EFT reduce physical and emotional pain, eliminate fear, stress, and anxiety, and help people transform things that they know in their heads to be true, into things that they know to be true in their hearts. I've seen it work, and therefore I'm less concerned with understanding why it successfully treats so many conditions, and instead am more concerned with finding ways to harness and apply its power.

The more I've learned, the more I can see, in my family, friends, and even strangers, ways that EFT could be used to heal emotional pain and trauma. A common refrain when talking to me, sometimes to the annoyance of my loved ones, has become, "You know, you should really tap on that!" I truly believe that learning and using this tool can change lives for the better.

*Introduction*

One of the areas where I've seen lots of opportunities for healing is in the gifted world. As the parent of a gifted child, I've spent quite a bit of time over the past several years with other families with gifted children; a few years ago, I even joined the leadership team of a non-profit designed to support profoundly gifted children and their families. I've learned a great deal about gifted development and education from world-renowned experts as well as the people in the trenches. I've heard the stories, read the books, and seen the faces of giftedness.

I've met a number of gifted children, many of whom are struggling to thrive despite their myriad abilities. I know a lot of parents who are doing everything in their power to support their gifted kids in a world that doesn't understand or assist them. I've seen families whose every interaction is shaped by the giftedness of their members, and I've seen individuals struggling to make sense of themselves and their worlds because they are different from normal, or more accurately, neurotypical, people. And while much of the story of giftedness is about triumph and joy, along the way, I've also seen great amounts of pain that I believe EFT could help to heal.

While I wrote this book specifically for the parents of gifted children, it can also be used by teachers or other caregivers, or even by gifted teens and children themselves. It discusses some of what I've learned the past fifteen years about giftedness, with a clear focus on the ways energy psychology can support gifted individuals.

The book is broken into four parts. Part One covers the basics of the Emotional Freedom Techniques, explaining how it heals emotional injuries and how it may benefit gifted individuals particularly, as well as how to do it. Part Two explores ways that EFT can be applied to some of the academic challenges of giftedness including boredom, imposter syndrome, and twice exceptionality. Part Three discusses how EFT can support some of the additional challenges facing gifted individuals, including perfectionism, anxiety, and depression. Each of these sections can be used by parents or teachers with the gifted children in their lives, or EFT can be taught directly to kids so they can use the tool themselves.

Part Four is directed specifically at the parents of gifted children. Children's characteristics come from their parents in some combination of nature and nurture, and it's common for children to experience many things that their parents also faced. This section is designed to help you, as the parent of a gifted child, heal yourself and your own past so that you can better support your children on their journeys.

It is my dearest wish that parents and teachers will learn to use the power of tapping to help gifted kids deal with the unique challenges of giftedness, tangibly improving the lives of those children and, by extension, all those who care about them.

PART ONE

# The Emotional Freedom Techniques

The Emotional Freedom Techniques is a quick, effective, and easy-to-use tool that heals emotional pain. It can be learned and used by anyone, and it can be a valuable tool to aid gifted children as they navigate the struggles and heartaches that come with being different from "normal."

*Tapping for the Gifted Child*

CHAPTER ONE

# Giftedness and the Emotional Freedom Techniques

Norah, not quite two years old, happily looked through her brand new picture book. On the page showing a bouquet of flowers, she pointed to each blossom in turn, correctly identifying blooms as yellow, red, pink, and purple. The next page depicted an airport, and she again moved her chubby finger around the drawing, identifying each part. "Airplane, grass, flag, windsock..."

Four-year-old Sam sat erect in his booster seat, looking out the back window of the family car. "Daddy, what's a tobacco shop?" he asked.

"It's a store where they sell things made from tobacco, like pipes and cigars. Why do you ask?"

"We just drove past one and I didn't know what it was," he answered.

Sam's father was surprised. He didn't know Sam knew how to read.

Eight-year-old Damian stormed into the house and burst into tears. For his birthday, he had gotten a kit to build his own ham radio and was eager to show it to the kids in his class. "But when I tried to show it to them," he said, "They just walked away." His lower lip trembled. "How come nobody likes me?"

Lauren's parents had enrolled her in the International Baccalaureate program in the local high school because they hoped she would finally be challenged, but so far, it wasn't working out. The curriculum followed a spiral design, covering broad topics several times over several years at increasing levels of complexity, but Lauren found this incredibly frustrating. She felt she was forever returning to old material instead of moving ahead, especially in math. "Mom?" she asked sadly. "Won't we *ever* get to differential equations?"

Norah, Sam, Damian, and Lauren are gifted. They have broad vocabularies, advanced interests, and a hunger to learn. They also feel varying levels of loneliness, frustration, and boredom, because they often can't connect to their age-peers and feel unsatisfied by their formal educations. Parents and teachers are frequently at a loss to help, because they don't always understand what sets these children apart nor how to support their unique development.

Many professionals believe there is a "sweet spot" in terms of child development, because children who are bright but not highly gifted often have the easiest time in school. Bright children find school to be challenging but not too challenging. They frequently have the right answer in class and do well on tests, while their developmental milestones and interests are about on par with their classmates. Bright children find school to be rewarding, and teachers generally find them to be a joy to teach.

Gifted children, on the other hand, don't always enjoy these advantages. Rather than finding school to be at just the right level of challenge, many find it to be far too easy. Rather than giving "correct" answers in class or on tests, they may give answers that are true but also creative, divergent, or out of the box. They may ask difficult, probing questions, and this may earn them a reputation as being troublesome. They may reach developmental milestones years ahead of other children their age, and their interests may vary widely from what is considered "normal." Being gifted isn't easy, and these children's challenges often affect the adults – parents, teachers, and others – who care about them. But it is possible to help them become happy, well-adjusted gifted adults.

## Giftedness

In academic and parenting circles, the term "gifted" is used to describe children whose academic abilities allow them to learn more quickly and retain information more easily than other children of the same age. Although this single term is used to describe them all, gifted children possess a wide variety of skills: They may have amazing abilities in math, write beautiful poetry, have advanced vocabularies or astonishing recall, thrive on puzzles or read voraciously. In all cases, what sets them apart is that in some areas, their abilities markedly exceed the abilities of more typical children of the same age.

It's not uncommon for these academic abilities to be the primary characteristics used to identify gifted individuals, which means the common view of giftedness is that it's solely about academic performance. However, there's a lot more to being gifted than just having a quick mind. Giftedness is actually a complex suite of characteristics, of which accelerated academic ability is just one.

Although a common misconception about gifted individuals is that their abilities are uniformly elevated, this is almost never true. In fact, one of the most defining characteristics of giftedness is the tendency to learn different material – including various academic subjects, social conventions, and physical skills – at different speeds. By definition, gifted children learn some material more quickly than their peers, but most gifted children develop in some areas at the same rate as their age peers, and it's even common for them to lag behind their agemates in other areas. In fact, this tendency to learn different material at different rates led the Columbus Group, a group of experts in giftedness, to coin the term "asynchronous learner" as an alternative to the term, "gifted."

The asynchronous learner ends up working on a variety of levels simultaneously, which can make it extremely challenging to support his or her growth and development. For example, it's possible that some highly gifted children may find themselves working on preschool fine motor skills, middle school emotional development, elementary school language skills and college level physics – simultaneously. It's easy to imagine how such a wide variety in abilities could make it extremely difficult for schools and parents to meet all of these different needs at the same time.

In addition to varying levels of academic prowess, the combination of characteristics which make up giftedness includes key emotional components. Although these emotional elements are seldom considered an integral part of giftedness by the general population, they are central to the gifted experience and significantly affect the lives of these individuals.

In many ways, the primary emotional aspect of giftedness is intensity. Indeed, gifted people are so frequently intense in both emotions and focus that intensity can almost be seen as synonymous with giftedness. From the child who "does nothing by halves," to the parent who sometimes feels as if they are living in the focus of a laser beam, the parents of gifted children commonly report intensity in their children's interests, feelings, and behaviors, and this intensity usually continues throughout life. Many parents and teachers find this intensity to be exhausting, because it takes a great deal of energy to engage with intense individuals, but intensity is generally a natural, inborn characteristic of gifted people.

Another natural trait of many gifted people is a deep concern with issues of fairness and justice, even at a young age. Gifted children may express great interest in religion, equality, or issues of right and wrong; however, this trait can lead to behaviors that may be challenging for both the child and those in his or her life. For example, sometimes a child's drive for justice can exasperate parents, teachers, and playmates alike, who may misunderstand it as a tendency to "tattle tale." Some parents are frustrated by the propensity of their gifted children to watch constantly for the slightest perceived unfairness in distributing family benefits, ranging from the serving size of dessert to the number of sleepovers in a year. Some gifted children are almost incapable of telling lies, and at times, their honesty may be interpreted as ill manners. It turns out that some of the individuals who are deeply concerned with fairness end up in careers in law or social justice, because their need to address injustice is such a driving force in their personalities; however, even if they end up working in other fields, many gifted individuals who possess this deep concern for justice maintain it throughout life. Concern with justice is a common lifelong characteristic of the gifted.

Many gifted children are concerned with justice in part because they possess two other common gifted traits: empathy and sensitivity. From an early age, many gifted kids are able to mentally put themselves in the place of others, and to imagine the pain others feel. Stories abound of gifted youngsters taking collections to support various charities, creating their own non-profit organizations to address societal needs, or becoming vegetarians in response to the treatment of commercial livestock. Moreover, many gifted children are intensely sensitive, so the pains and injustices of the world may affect them more deeply than they do other children of the same age. They may weep easily when seeing someone suffer, or they may need to avoid common books or cartoons because they contain too much fictional violence for the child to handle. Strong empathy and emotional sensitivity are common among the gifted, and as with other emotional traits of giftedness, may remain heightened throughout life.

    Yet there's even more to giftedness than increased academic ability and various emotional traits. The brain changes that cause faster learning and emotional differences also frequently result in increased sensitivity to stimuli of every sort. Gifted people may feel that lights are too bright, noises too loud, or flavors too strong, or they may be sensitive to stimuli that others may not even notice – the scent of a person which lingers in a room long after that person has departed, for example. Gifted individuals may be more sensitive to environmental stimuli of other sorts as well; they may also experience increased incidents of allergies to foods or environmental triggers. Again, the experience of being gifted is often far more complex than simply learning quickly.

In addition to these many differences from the general population, gifted individuals differ from one another, as well. Giftedness exists in a continuum, from the individuals who learn somewhat more quickly than their age peers, to those who exhibit dramatically advanced learning skills. In the literature, the common terms used to describe different levels of ability are Gifted, Highly Gifted, Exceptionally Gifted, and finally Profoundly Gifted.

As a rule, the more gifted the individual, the more likely the person is to have life experiences which differ significantly from the lives of neurotypical people. It's common, although not universal, for increasing levels of giftedness to be accompanied by increasing levels of intensity, asynchrony, sensitivity, and other traits of giftedness; thus, it's not unusual to find that with increasing levels of giftedness comes an increased need for support. However, because relatively few people are familiar with the levels of giftedness, the differing needs of gifted learners may not be addressed, and some gifted children may not get the support they require.

Another reason gifted children may not get the support they need to be successful is that it is possible to be gifted and to simultaneously have one or more disabilities, including learning disabilities. In the gifted world, individuals who are both gifted and suffering from learning disabilities such as dyslexia or dyscalculia are not unusual. These people are commonly called 2E, or twice exceptional, because their abilities are exceptionally advanced in some areas and exceptionally delayed in others. Nor does giftedness protect against other mental or physical disorders. Giftedness can coexist with depression, ADHD, vision and hearing problems, OCD, narcissism, and more.

These various, sometimes seemingly conflicting, traits within the gifted population can lead to social isolation, boredom in school, anxiety or depression. People in the wider community who hear the term "gifted" frequently think, "These kids are smart. They can take care of themselves." But parents who are trying to raise children with these characteristics know that it is often a hard, lonely road. Despite popular misconceptions, gifted children are at no lower risk than the general population of dropping out of school, using drugs, or committing suicide. They *do* need support, because virtually all gifted individuals feel misunderstood on some level simply because they see the world differently.

Although there are benefits that accompany the ability to master some material with ease relative to the norm, giftedness is a multi-faceted experience, and learning quickly is not a magic ticket to an easy life. Being gifted doesn't protect one from the slings and arrows of life, and emotional injuries are as common and damaging for gifted individuals as they are for anyone else.

## Emotional Injuries

Just as our bodies may be injured by violence, so, too, are our emotions vulnerable to damage. Although the term "emotional injury" is most commonly associated with personal injury lawsuits, emotional injuries affect everyone. From time to time, everyone experiences emotional distress ranging from small upsets to great trauma, and some of these injuries can produce significant and lasting pain. While emotional injuries affect everyone, gifted children may be particularly prone to emotional damage. They may experience emotional harm for reasons and from sources that neurotypical individuals simply don't encounter.

One frequent cause of emotional injury for the gifted is the disparity between their mental and emotional processing capabilities. As a rule, children generally tune out material they don't understand, but gifted children's intellectual abilities will often allow them to understand conversations and follow news reports that other children disregard. It's common, therefore, for gifted kids to have exposure to topics such as global warming, human trafficking, or death, long before they're ready to deal with these issues on an emotional level. When children mentally understand situations they cannot process emotionally, they often experience great, and frequently sustained, distress. These emotional injuries can lead to great suffering and even existential depression at very young ages, which may persist for years.

Another frequent source of emotional injury in the gifted is their heightened emotional sensitivity, which often leads gifted kids to experience pain at times when neurotypical children do not. Many parents of gifted children find that their kids cannot read the same books or watch the same television programs as their classmates, because even a passing reference to painful material causes their children too much distress. This was an issue my family really struggled with, because even when I would pre-read books and think they would be acceptable, my daughter would often still be hurt by some element of the plot that hadn't even registered with me. For example, I once gave her a book to read while I met with a gifted professional about her education. I had read the book and thought it would keep her happily busy during my meeting, but when I checked on her a short while later, I found her sobbing quietly in a corner, because it was briefly mentioned that the main character's mother had died – an incident she still refers to many years later as, "The *Despereaux* Debacle." Indeed, many parents of gifted children really struggle to find appropriate reading material for their kids, because the children want to read books with complex plots and advanced vocabularies, but books with these characteristics often include events which overwhelm gifted readers. Their highly sensitive natures can cause these children to experience emotional injuries from seemingly benign sources.

  At other times, gifted children's empathy may lead to emotional trauma through vicarious experiences. Empathetic gifted children don't have to personally experience something to feel emotional repercussions from an event. For example, they may feel guilty for another child's misbehavior, even if the child who perpetrated the act feels none. It is common for gifted children to feel deep pain when siblings or friends are punished for wrongdoing, even if they themselves have done nothing wrong and have not been punished, or they may feel acute embarrassment for the social faux pas of others. Although empathy is a desirable personality trait, in its extreme forms, it can be tremendously painful for gifted individuals to bear.

Regardless of the source of the damage, there are several ways to respond to emotional wounds, but too often, people rely on unhealthy methods to deal with their pain. Sometimes we admit our pain, but this vulnerable response may be ill-judged in emotionally dangerous situations and may lead to further hurt. For instance, many children have said, "You hurt my feelings!" only to have other children laugh at them, causing further damage. At other times, we may deny our emotional injuries, lying to others about the hurt we feel, or we may repress them, lying even to ourselves about the extent of our suffering. While these are natural and even instinctive reactions to emotional injury, none of these responses actually reduce the pain we feel, nor do they prevent it from becoming an ongoing problem.

Sometimes, we're taught to deal with our pain in more productive ways. For example, cognitive behavioral therapy, teaches us that our emotions result from our thoughts. By identifying the ways our thinking is distorted, we can correct our thoughts and thus correct our feelings. While this can be useful in some situations, overreliance on this tool teaches us to "fix" our emotions or to rationalize our feelings away, rather than truly healing them.

Alternatively, we may be taught to use tools such as visualization, meditation, psychoanalysis, or hypnosis, and each of these may be helpful for some individuals at various times. However, using these instruments may require specialized expertise, and even they aren't always reliable ways to reduce emotional suffering. Even healthy techniques may not fully clear emotional damage.

Unfortunately, emotional injuries can remain for a long time. They say time heals all wounds, but some emotional wounds never heal, and continue to inflict pain every time we remember them. Others are regularly called to mind by our lives or environments, and thus we live much of our lives re-experiencing the pain of an old injury. Time doesn't necessarily erase the suffering associated with emotional hurts.

Thankfully, there is another tool that can be used to heal emotional damage: the Emotional Freedom Techniques, also called EFT or "tapping" due to how it is performed. This technique was developed over the past few decades, and is a safe way to release painful emotions, whether caused by an event that happened today or years ago. It affects negative emotions without disrupting positive ones, and in its basic form can be used by practically anyone. It is a valuable tool in mending emotional damage.

## How EFT Can Help with Gifted Issues

If you've read this far, you probably recognize your family in these pages. You may have first-hand experience with the joys of giftedness, but you're probably also grappling with some of its downsides. Know that you're not alone, and your family's pain is real. There really are problems which are unique to, or at least more prevalent in, gifted populations, and if your family is facing one or more of these issues, you and your children are suffering. I may not know your precise circumstances, but I *know* your pain is real. I also know it doesn't have to be this way. It *is* possible for gifted families to live without pain. There are ways to approach common problems which can reduce your family's suffering, and EFT is one tool that addresses the downsides of being gifted.

The most important way that EFT aids gifted families is by helping to heal emotional pain and trauma. Although the disadvantages of being gifted aren't always widely recognized, that makes them no less real. Because EFT can be used to heal most any negative emotion, it can be applied to a variety of stresses, disappointments, fears, and painful memories, from phobias to shame to generalized anxiety. It helps gifted individuals navigate the trials and heartaches that come with being different from the norm.

Once the tool has been mastered, its flexibility gives families a single, reliable instrument to reduce suffering in almost any circumstance. It can reduce the pain of everything from failed tests to broken hearts to fights with siblings. A common phrase in the tapping world is, "Try it on everything!" because EFT addresses all manner of negative emotions and even physical pains, to the point where even long-time tappers are still sometimes surprised by its effectiveness. EFT is a single tool that is flexible enough to work on all kinds of pain.

Many people find the simple act of performing EFT to be comforting for a variety of reasons. Its repetitive nature can be soothing, because there is a familiar rhythm involved in tapping through regular points over and over. EFT includes empathetic elements that invite people to slow down and focus on exactly how they feel, and it provides individuals with a sense of control, because the ability to offer tangible relief during times of distress helps people feel empowered. People of all ages find that doing EFT can become a comforting routine during times of suffering.

Another way EFT can benefit families is that while it can be used with a certified practitioner, it doesn't have to be. Its basic form can be learned by most anyone and applied by laypeople without special training. Parents, teachers, and other caregivers can use this tool to support the children in their lives in meaningful ways, without having to rely on outside experts and without investing hours in therapeutic training. Children can even be taught to use the tool themselves. EFT is available to everyone.

EFT is also useful because of its portability and immediacy. It can be used pretty much anywhere, because there is no special equipment required. Moreover, a round of EFT can be completed in less than five minutes, and it often reduces your child's distress substantially in that time. Parents and teachers can learn to use tapping to respond quickly to children's crises to help children to calm down and reduce their suffering in both the short and long terms.

Another advantage to EFT is that it reduces or eliminates painful emotions without affecting positive ones. Unlike some medications, for example, EFT is able to reduce children's pain without curtailing their joy and exuberance. The theory behind EFT states that emotions are created by the body's energy being in motion, and negative emotions are created when that energy is blocked by some negative event. EFT eliminates energetic blocks, allowing energy to flow freely again, which in turn removes negative feelings. By contrast, positive emotions are the result of freely flowing energy, and because there are no blockages involved, tapping on those emotions literally can't change anything. Because it doesn't interfere with positive emotions, parents and teachers can use tapping without fear of creating negative outcomes.

EFT helps to heal old emotional wounds and to successfully manage emotional upsets as they happen, which are gifts beyond measure for any child, not only a gifted one. But because being gifted comes with so many different, extra ways for emotional wounds to develop, EFT is a particularly valuable tool when parenting or teaching a gifted child.

## Not the Only Solution

Although EFT is often extremely beneficial when dealing with the emotional strains that accompany giftedness, it is not a panacea. Helping gifted children learn strategies to minimize their pain is a great first step, but they may need more than pain relief. Many gifted children need systemic, structural changes in their lives to relieve their suffering long term, so parents may want to investigate all areas of their children's lives to see what adjustments would be helpful. For instance, children may benefit from a change in their school or social environments, or they may need outside support from an occupational therapist or mental health counselor. Regardless of what changes are needed, EFT can be a helpful adjunct to a suite of solutions that support gifted children as they grow.

CHAPTER TWO

# What to Do and What to Expect

One reason some people find EFT to be a "woo-woo" tool is because at first blush, it looks a little like stereotypical images of witchcraft. It seems that you say some magic words, make a few ritualized gestures, and suddenly, so the story goes, all your problems disappear. In reality, EFT isn't like that. The words aren't magic, the movements are simple and straightforward, and the results may take anywhere from a few minutes to several sessions to appear.

In EFT, words and movements work together to clear what are called emotional blockages. Positive emotions are created by the movement of the body's energy, whereas negative emotions are created when that energy is blocked by some negative event. Tapping eliminates energetic blocks, allowing energy to flow freely again and thereby removing those negative feelings.

In some ways, EFT is like using a smart phone or tablet. Touching a specific place on a screen will have one effect in one application, but touching the exact same place will produce a very different result in a different app. With tapping, the issues we focus on, and the words we use to control that focus, are like the applications on a tablet. Touching one point while focusing on one issue will clear one thing, but touching the exact same place while focusing on something else will clear something entirely different. The words and movements work together to address a wide variety of issues.

The process is simple to learn, but it can take time to master the nuances. Here's what you need to know to get started:

## The Movements

The movements of EFT are designed to stimulate acupressure points on the body. Most people tap gently on these points seven or eight times with the tips of two or three fingers. You may also gently massage these points with your fingertips, which is especially helpful for people who are sensitive to touch.

Remember to be gentle with yourself. Tapping harder does not make the process more effective, and many times these points are very sensitive and may be sore after tapping as a consequence of clearing old blockages. Use firm but gentle pressure for EFT.

Generally speaking, one moves from upper to lower points on the body, finishing the tapping sequence on the top of the head; however, you can adjust the routine to suit your, or your child's, preferences. Many people feel more of an affinity to some points than to others, or they may feel an aversion to tapping certain areas. You can choose to tap twice on a preferred point or leave one out of your routine altogether. Trust yourself and follow your instincts.

## The Points

There are a number of acupressure points on the head and torso conventionally used in EFT. These points may be tender or even painful to the touch, so use gentle pressure when looking for them. In many cases, you'll know you've found the correct place when you find a spot that is sensitive to the touch. Note that you don't have to tap precisely on the point every time. Tapping gently in the immediate vicinity of the point is usually sufficient.

The body is symmetrical, so there are matching points on both sides of the body unless the point is located in the exact center of the body, as under the nose. You can tap on whichever side appeals to you more. It's fine to alternate sides, or to tap on one side of the body using the opposite hand. Many people choose to tap on both sides of the body simultaneously. Figure out and use the tapping technique that feels comfortable for you.

These are the acupressure points we're going to use in this book:

1. **Above the eye, also called the eyebrow point:** Touch the end of the eyebrow nearest the nose, then move up toward the forehead about one finger-width to where the brow ridge meets the plane of the forehead.
2. **Side of the eye:** Touch the outer edge of the eyebrow, where the bone of the skull connects to the softer tissue of the temple, and slide the finger down about a half a finger width so that your fingers

are beside your eye socket. Wearers of eyeglasses may need to remove them to reach this point.

3. **Under the eye:** Touch the area below the middle of the eye and slide the finger upward to where the bone ends at the eye socket. When pressing gently on the bone directly under the eye, you'll find a small notch in the bone. You want to tap this notch. Again, people who wear eyeglasses may need to remove them to reach this point.

4. **Under the nose:** This point is located in the center of the indentation above your upper lip.

5. **Under the mouth, also called the chin point:** Touch the center of the deepest part of the indentation of the chin, midway between the lower lip and the bottom of the chin. Some people prefer to use fingernails to reach this area, as it is recessed and can be hard to access.

6. **Collarbone:** Follow your collarbone toward the center of your chest where the two clavicles almost come together, then move your finger down from the end of the collarbone about an inch. Be careful with this point – most people initially look too far toward the side of the body, or too low on the chest. This point is high and near the center of the body.

7. **Under the arm:** Put your hand in your armpit and slide about one hand width down the middle of your side as seen from front to back. This point is about where the bra strap would be on a woman and is frequently extremely tender.

8. **Top of the head:** There are a variety of points on the top of the head, so when tapping here, move the hand across both sides of the crown on the head.
9. **Karate chop point, also called side of the hand:** This point is located on the side of the hand between the base of the pinky finger and the outside of the wrist.

These points are shown in the photo in Figure 1.

*Figure 1. Tapping points*

There are a number of other points on the body that can be used during tapping. If you meet with an EFT practitioner, he or she may employ these points for various reasons; in particular, there are a number of points near the fingernails which are often used in the long form of EFT.

Interestingly, it turns out that people will naturally stimulate many of these points to soothe themselves when they are stressed or upset. People may massage their temples, stimulating the Side of the Eye point, or may rub their eyes, which may stimulate the Above the Eye, Side of the Eye, and Under the Eye points simultaneously. Similarly, people may wring their hands or bite their fingernails, which stimulates the finger points. People instinctively know that touching these areas of the body can be calming.

## The Words

Although it is possible to do effective EFT without saying a word, the words spoken during an EFT session serve to focus the attention of the person tapping on the issue being addressed. Many people find that their minds will wander if they tap without speaking. By saying words that draw the attention back to the issue at each tapping point, tappers can ensure that they stay on track and address the issue thoroughly.

Language is important, because the words we use reflect the thoughts we have. When using EFT, it's important to use language that "lands" with you. One person may refer to their offspring as a "child," while another may naturally use the term, "kid." It's important that the language feels as natural as possible to the person tapping, so as to most closely reflect his or her subconscious thoughts. When using the sample routines presented in this book, feel free to adjust the words so they sound like the person who is tapping.

Similarly, the suggested tapping routines are, by their nature, very general. EFT works better the more specific you can be, so you should feel free to substitute more specific words for less specific ones. Using names, places, and other details can help to clear issues much more quickly than a non-specific routine can do. Many of the sample routines in this book include places where specific language would be beneficial, and these areas are called out using brackets and italics *[like this]* so you know when to insert your own details.

Many EFT routines begin with what is called the setup phrase, and all suggested routines in this book will include this step. The setup is a two-part phrase, repeated three times while tapping on the karate chop point. The first part of the setup is to acknowledge the problem. Most commonly, this sounds something like, "Even though I have this issue..." For example, "Even though I was hurt by what my teacher said..." or "Even though I felt left out when the other kids played a game I don't like..." The second part of the setup is some sort of personal acceptance or validation, such as, "... I love and accept myself anyway," or "... I accept myself and how I feel about this."

For many people, saying the second part of the setup phrase can be difficult, especially at first. We're often not explicitly taught to love ourselves and may struggle to see ourselves in a positive light. Yet these words are crucial to the success of EFT for several reasons. First, accepting ourselves along with our issues gives us control over those problems. When we deny that we have a problem, or believe there is something wrong with us for even *having* an issue, we aren't in a mindset that allows us to heal that issue. We have to own the story before we can write the ending we want. Second, it's important to practice self-acceptance and self-love regardless of what problems we have. When we base our self-worth on the expectation of being perfect, which is unachievable, we may set ourselves up for lifelong problems.

For people who are simply unable to say, "I deeply and completely love and accept myself," it's fine to use variations on this theme. "I want to accept and love myself," "I'm trying to see myself in a better light," or even, "I accept that I cannot accept myself at this time," are acceptable statements. The goal is simply to acknowledge that we are worthwhile human beings, despite the weaknesses that we sometimes struggle to overcome.

After saying the setup phrase three times while tapping the karate chop point, the routine then moves through each of the other points in turn, speaking a reminder phrase while tapping gently at each point before moving on. The reminder can be extremely simple, such as, "What the teacher said," repeated at each point, or the routine may be a little more sophisticated in an attempt to ferret out more of the emotional distress surrounding each issue. The routines presented in this book use somewhat more varied language at each point to try to heal more of the emotions around each issue.

Generally, routines will conclude at a point where the person tapping feels things come together. For many people, the Top of the Head is such a point, and the routines presented in this book will conclude at this point. Once you know your own body and how you respond to the various acupressure points, you can choose to finish your routines on the point that seems to help you clear your issues most.

## Measuring Distress

EFT practitioners commonly measure their clients' distress using the SUDs scale, or the Subjective Units of Distress. This scale was created in the 1960s and is used extensively in clinical and therapeutic settings to allow a suffering person to quantify his or her discomfort. The scale runs from 10 – the most painful experience imaginable – down to 0, when no discomfort is felt at all. Taking a SUDs score both before and after performing a round of EFT allows you to know when shifts have taken place and when events have cleared completely.

Changes in SUDs levels are not linear with EFT. While it is possible that tapping through a single EFT sequence will clear an issue, it's also possible that no change will occur with a single round of EFT. Sometimes, you may experience a small amount of relief and need to

## What to Do and What to Expect

repeat a sequence using slightly different words. It's even possible that a SUDs score will increase after a round or two, which is usually a signal that you've triggered memories of other, related issues. Continued work on the topic, using different words if necessary, should bring relief. If you can't seem to get a problem to clear, check out *When EFT Doesn't Work* at the end of this chapter.

### Putting It All Together

Despite what it may sound like, EFT isn't really confusing once you try it, so let's put all this together and give it a try with an extremely simple sample routine.

First, find the acupressure points previously described, so you'll know where to tap once you get started. Next, think of a painful time in your life when you felt left out that still bothers you today – it can be in school, in your family of origin, or at work – and give that event a SUDs score. Now, begin tapping, consistently but gently on each point in turn, while you speak the following words aloud:

| Point | Statement |
| --- | --- |
| *Karate chop* | Even though I felt left out, I accept myself anyway. |
|  | Even though I felt left out that day, I completely accept myself. |
|  | Even though I felt left out, I deeply and completely love and accept myself. |
| *Above the eye* | I felt left out. |

35

| Point | Statement |
|---|---|
| Side of the eye | I felt so left out. |
| Under the eye | And it hurt. |
| Under the nose | I wanted to belong. |
| Under the mouth | I wanted to be accepted, but I wasn't. |
| Collarbone | I acknowledge now how much it hurt. |
| Under the arm | And I choose to let it go. |
| Top of the head | I release my hurt so I can know peace. |

Now take a deep, slow breath in through your nose, hold it for a second, and release it slowly through your mouth. That's it. After you exhale, reevaluate the initial event and give it an updated SUDs score. If your SUDs level has changed, you've had your very first emotional shift thanks to EFT. Congratulations!

## Your Own Routines

This book includes many sample tapping routines to help you start using EFT immediately, but these suggestions are by no means exhaustive. Once you get a feel for the process, it's possible for you to create routines tailored directly to you and your issues.

### Scripts

For many people, particularly those who are new to EFT, thinking about which words to say while simultaneously tapping the points can feel overwhelming. To help you get started, this book provides sample scripts that you can read aloud while you tap along. When you're ready, you can create written scripts of your own prior to tapping, separating the creation of the words from the execution of the routine.

Formulas

Whether or not you write down what you want to say before you begin to tap, it's often wise to use "formulas" to deal with certain issues. Formulas ensure you cover all the salient aspects of a problem and don't leave out anything important.

For example, using a three-part formula can be very helpful to clear painful emotions. In the first part, acknowledge the emotion – call it by name, call it by synonyms and alternate names, and otherwise really own the feeling. For instance, at different points in turn, you might say, "Betrayed. I feel betrayed. I've been stabbed in the back. I feel hurt so-and-so would do this to me. I can't believe they would do this. I am outraged! Who do they think they are, betraying me?"

In the second part, validate the emotion. So often in life, we are told what we "should" feel. When the way we actually *do* feel runs counter to these expectations, we deny, repress, or in some way try to pretend we don't feel the way we do. And yet, it's important to acknowledge that our feelings are valid, no matter what they are. For example, "And it's okay that I feel betrayed. Anyone would feel betrayed in my shoes. I can feel betrayed for the rest of my life if I want to!"

In the third part, release the emotion. While our feelings are perfectly acceptable, no matter what they are, that doesn't mean that it serves us to hold onto them. Frequently, we're best off when we acknowledge how we feel and then just allow that emotion to pass out of our systems. For example, "And so, even though this feeling of betrayal is valid, I'm choosing to let it go now. I'm choosing to release my anger. I'm choosing to release my hurt. I'm choosing to know that I'm okay, no matter how so-and-so behaved. I'm choosing to let my resentment go, because I deserve to heal."

### Free-Form EFT

Neither scripts nor formulas are necessary to perform successful EFT. Once the setup phrase has been created, you can simply say whatever words come to mind as you think about the issue you're working on, tapping through the points as you go.

Don't be surprised to find that your mind may range all over when doing free-form EFT. Although you may start by working very specifically on one issue, you may find other words, ideas, or issues coming to the surface as you progress. Our brains link together ideas that seem to be related, and those related ideas can be called to mind as we work through issues using EFT. This isn't necessarily a problem, because you're allowing yourself to work through all related aspects of the issue, but sometimes we find ourselves following so many tangents that we never seem to clear the original issue. If you find this is true for you, you may wish to keep paper and pencil nearby when you tap so you can make note of the related ideas that come to mind. This will enable you to follow those tangential thoughts at a later time while still focusing on the issue you started with until you feel it shift.

## Practitioners

If you find that you or your child aren't making the progress you hoped for, or that things just don't seem to be clearing in the way you expected, you may wish to work with a practitioner trained in the use of EFT. This person can create detailed routines to help you clear painful memories and can help you to identify and clear the core issues and limiting beliefs that are being brought to the surface by your experiences. Sometimes, simply adding the energy and perspective of another person to a tapping situation can allow stubborn blockages to clear. An EFT practitioner can offer an empathetic mirror for your experiences, and that validation can sometimes help your emotions to release more easily. Although it's not necessary to use a practitioner to gain the benefits of EFT, there are times when they are helpful.

The process of clearing one blocked emotion is much like clearing any other blocked emotion, so EFT practitioners can easily work on issues ranging from phobias to cravings to PTSD. However, many practitioners choose to work with specific populations, and you may want to find someone who specializes in the issues you are working to clear. These practitioners will possess greater experience with many aspects of the issue you or your family are facing; they may also be more accustomed to working with people like you. A practitioner who has extensive experience with combat veterans may not be as comfortable working with children, and vice versa.

### Personal and Private Issues

There may be times when you or your children are dealing with events that are too painful to talk about comfortably, but that doesn't mean that you cannot use EFT to heal them, nor does it mean you cannot work with a professional practitioner.

EFT doesn't need to be done aloud in order to be effective. If you are working with a professional, they will be able to utilize techniques that allow you or your child to work silently on the situation in question. If you are working with your child yourself, you can invite your child to tap through the points while *thinking* about a problem rather than talking about it. If desired, you can prompt them at each point to think of the relevant details, including what happened next, how they felt, or what other details they can recall. Thus, you can help them stay on track with their tapping even if they don't tell you – or your professional of choice – about what happened.

### What to Expect

When an issue has been fully resolved using EFT, people report feeling that the emotional distress they felt previously is "just gone." Although they can remember the details of an event, they no longer feel pain when thinking of it, and they may not even remember why that event caused them grief in the past. They may feel lighter, or more at ease. They may also experience cognitive shifts which allow them to see an event from a different perspective. They may understand the viewpoint of another person, or may suddenly not care about the motivations of another person, although they used to care

## What to Do and What to Expect

deeply about, "Why did they do that?" Their SUDs level will drop substantially, often to zero.

In addition to emotional reactions to the process, the body also has a number of physical responses to clearing issues during EFT. While tapping, don't be surprised to find that you or your children do some of the following: burp, sigh, yawn, cry, laugh, shake, hiccup, or even pass gas. Also, in the hours or days that follow an intense EFT session, you may experience exhaustion or a need to sleep; soreness at the acupressure points; or intestinal distress, such as an upset stomach or diarrhea. The stronger your negative emotions were before they cleared, the more likely you are to experience side effects after the session, and the more intense your reaction is likely to be.

If your response seems severe or doesn't fade within a day or so, contact an EFT practitioner for guidance. It's possible that you may have missed aspects of an event during tapping and a bit of clean up will allow you to fully release the event and find relief.

### When EFT Doesn't Work

Sometimes, EFT just doesn't seem to work. People will tap through a routine without any feeling of clearing, and they may change the words and try again to no avail. If this happens, don't despair. There are a few things you can try to get past plateaus.

First, drink water. EFT works through your energy system, and the electrical impulses in your body, like all electrical impulses, will flow more easily in a hydrated environment.

Second, be emphatic in your speech. You might yell rather than speak the words, or use an imperative tone of voice. You want what you are saying to register with even the resistant parts of your brain.

Third, try using more specific language in your routine. Add as many details as you can about events that happened, including information from as many of your five senses as fits the situation. You can even include what you thought at a given moment. EFT works best when it is specific.

Resistance

At times, the person tapping subconsciously won't allow EFT to work. This person may have subconscious resistance to releasing the issue they are working on, not because they are bad or stupid, but because some part of themselves believes it is safer or better to hold on to the belief, behavior, or memory in question than to let it go.

There are many reasons someone might resist clearing an issue. For example, some people resist letting memories go because the experiences have become part of their identities. They will describe themselves as, "I'm a person who..." and they don't want to let that go, because it's scary to change *who they are*. Sometimes, they don't want to lose a connection to someone, even a painful one, or to give up a dream, such as the dream of finally getting an apology. People may also resist healing because they fear that in so doing, they're condoning someone's behavior. If what happened was *wrong*, they don't want to just let that go, particularly if they are concerned with justice, as many gifted people are.

At other times, people experience what is called secondary gain; they get something good from something "bad" and thus resist giving it up. For example, although someone might complain about using a wheelchair, he or she might secretly love the attention the wheelchair brings and would therefore never willingly give it up.

It is possible to use EFT to release the resistance someone feels to clearing an issue. Working directly on resistance allows the tapper to find and acknowledge hidden incentives to hold onto a memory or emotion, and then help their subconscious mind to see that they don't need to hold on to it after all. This free-form version of tapping can be extremely powerful in removing the blocks that prevent one from moving forward with healing.

If you find yourself tapping diligently on an issue without result, you may wish to try the following. The script can only get you started, because the issues that come up vary by person. However, it should allow you to begin the process of exploring your resistance to healing. Remember to change the words in italics to specific words that reflect the situation you're working with.

| *Point* | Statement |
|---|---|
| *Karate chop* | Even though I'm not sure I'm ready to let *{this}* go, I accept how I feel and who I am. |

| Point | Statement |
|---|---|
| | Even though I'm not sure I want to deal with *{this issue}*, I love and accept myself anyway.<br><br>Even though I'm not ready to let *{this}* go, I deeply and completely love, accept, and forgive myself. |
| Above the eye | I'm not sure I'm ready to let this go. |
| Side of the eye | I'm not sure I want to deal with it at all. |
| Under the eye | It hurt so much when it happened. |
| Under the nose | And I'm not sure I'm ready to get past it. |
| Under the mouth | There's a part of me that wants to hold on to *{this memory or emotion}*. |
| Collarbone | There's a part of me that feels like I need to hold on to it. |
| Under the arm | Not because there's anything wrong with me. |
| Top of the head | My mind thinks it has good reason to hold on to this experience. |
| Above the eye | It thinks it's doing me a favor. |
| Side of the eye | And I love and appreciate the part of me that is trying to keep me safe. |
| Under the eye | Part of me wants to hold onto this experience because… |
| Under the nose | I'm afraid if I let it go, *{this}* will happen. |
| Under the mouth | I can't let that happen. It doesn't feel *{safe/ right/ something else}*. |
| Collarbone | And so I'm holding on. |

| Point | Statement |
|---|---|
| Under the arm | But is holding on to {this experience} really serving my best interests? |
| Top of the head | Might I be better served to let it go? |
| Above the eye | What would my life be like without {this}? |
| Side of the eye | I may never get the resolution I want. |
| Under the eye | But my suffering doesn't affect {other people}. |
| Under the nose | Right now, I'm the one who's suffering for holding on to {this}. |
| Under the mouth | So I'm opening myself to the possibility of letting it go. |
| Collarbone | I'm open to the possibility of healing. |
| Under the arm | I can choose to forgive {other people} or not. |
| Top of the head | But I'm choosing right now to set myself free. |
| *Take a deep breath in through your nose...* | |
| *Hold it for a few seconds...* | |
| *Release it slowly through your mouth.* | |

## It Can't Hurt to Try It

EFT is a very forgiving tool; perhaps the greatest issue that arises from its common use is that it may do nothing at all. If it's used for issues which it cannot affect, it won't have an effect. If it's applied too generally, or without fully acknowledging how you currently feel, EFT may not shift your emotional state. Truly, it's virtually impossible for EFT to harm someone who taps on everyday issues.

In fact, although there are many ways to make it more effective and efficient, doing just about any tapping will frequently provide positive results. It's not uncommon for people using this tool to feel empowered, because they're able to do something to affect their own health and well-being, and this alone can reduce feelings of distress. Also, for many children who have learned the tool, the familiarity of EFT can be very comforting, as can the validation of negative emotions. It can be very healing for children to be told that no matter *how* they feel in this moment, they're fine as they are, and then be guided gently to a less painful emotional state. Plus, studies have shown that even beginners to EFT reduce their blood cortisol levels by tapping, dropping their stress levels and feeling more relaxed (Church, Yount, & Brooks, 2012). Even stimulating the acupressure points without using words can be soothing for many people.

Moreover, the number of issues which EFT *does* affect is nearly limitless. It's common to hear professionals advise people to try EFT on everything, because our emotions play a large role in how our bodies, minds, and spirits function. Healing our emotions has profound, often unanticipated, benefits in all areas of our lives.

Remember that you don't have to believe in tapping for it to work. I once heard EFT described as the anti-placebo effect. The placebo effect is when someone tells us something will work, we believe it will work, and we see positive results. With EFT, however, the situation is often precisely the opposite. People are told it will work, they don't believe it for a second, and then it works anyway! Don't be afraid to try it, even if it seems bizarre or unlikely to work. You have nothing to lose but your pain.

CHAPTER THREE

# Triggering

"Triggering" is a psychological concept that will come up repeatedly throughout this book. Understanding triggering allows us to realize why some things bother us as much as they do, as well as why EFT can be so beneficial, not only by clearing acute distress, but also by dramatically reducing the recurrence of painful incidents in the future.

Triggering is when a current event reminds us, often subconsciously, of some traumatic event from our past, and *we respond to the previous event rather than the current one*. Often when people are triggered, they will react in ways that seem out of proportion to the current stimulus, or they will respond to something that didn't actually happen. However, for the person being triggered, whatever just occurred has reminded them of some previous encounter, and they are responding now in a way that would have been appropriate to that earlier event.

The trigger itself is whatever brings the previous situation to mind, and it can take just about any form, from the words someone says, to the situation in which we find ourselves, to the sensory input we get from our environments, such as a particular odor or the quality of the light. However, unless we are extremely aware, we rarely recognize our own triggers. We don't notice that we always become irritable or sad or afraid when exposed to certain stimuli; triggering takes place entirely outside our conscious awareness.

Not all triggering situations are negative. Although the term is used in psychological circles to refer to the experience of having a traumatic memory activated by something in our environment, it's also true that environmental stimuli can trigger positive memories. For example, tasting a favorite food from childhood may bring our loved ones to mind, or the smell of the ocean may remind us of a special vacation. In fact, there are entire industries devoted to positive triggering. Triggering is what makes us cry when we hear certain songs or when watching sentimental movies. It's not the movie itself that makes us cry, but that it reminds us of our first love or our dearly departed grandma. The movie triggers some old memory.

While some triggering situations are pleasant, others bring up strong negative emotions. People may find themselves feeling overwhelming fear, anger, or shame, and they will react accordingly. However, although the *reaction* to a trigger may be public and even dramatic, triggering itself is a subconscious process that happens entirely within the mind of the person being triggered. The brain relies on a small area called the amygdala to link together experiences that are similar in some way, and then to call those previous experiences instantly to mind when a related event takes place. This instantaneous recall evolved to help us respond to potential threats without the delay of conscious thought, and thus, triggering serves a beneficial purpose.

Imagine that ten thousand years ago, you were a child who watched a saber-toothed tiger bring down a giant elk. You would have heard the cries of the elk, smelled the blood of the animal, and you would have experienced some level of trauma from this event. You would have learned that this particular saber-toothed tiger is dangerous, and then your amygdala would have generalized a lesson from this experience. It would have decided that *all* saber-toothed tigers are dangerous, and perhaps you'd even have expanded that idea to include big cats of any kind. And for the rest of your life, seeing a big cat would instantly trigger subconscious memories of the day you watched the saber-toothed tiger bring down the giant elk, and you'd immediately get as far away from the cat as you could.

However, this behavior isn't always beneficial. Imagine now that you're giving an oral report in sixth grade and forget what you're supposed to say. Your classmates laugh at you, which activates instinctive, primal fears of being ejected from the group and forced to fend for yourself. Your brain will record this as a traumatic event and will generalize one or more lessons from this trauma. It may decide that sixth grade is dangerous, which can make the rest of the school year quite dreadful, or that these particular people are dangerous, which can carry over for all the years you are in school with these classmates.

Your brain may even decide that speaking in front of a group is dangerous, and that could affect you for the rest of your life. There may come a time when, as an adult, you are required for work to give a presentation, yet when you stand in front of the group, it triggers immediate, subconscious memories of that day back in the sixth grade when the other kids laughed at you. Rather than seeing yourself surrounded by curious coworkers, you react as though you are facing a hostile crowd whose objective is to oust you from the group and threaten your very existence. Being triggered would definitely not serve you well in this instance.

Everyone is triggered now and again, but because there are many times when it's counterproductive, it's important to learn how to recognize when it's happening and to learn techniques that will allow you to alleviate both the immediate distress as well as to lessen the frequency of negative triggering experiences in the future.

## What It Looks Like

Triggering happens so far outside our conscious awareness that it's common for people to not even realize that they've *been* triggered until they're in the throes of their reaction. Indeed, many people don't realize they've been triggered even then, and it's only the people around them who recognize that their behavior seems off.

The most common indication that someone has been triggered is that they will react in ways that seem out of proportion to the current stimulus. They may blow up or freak out over seemingly trivial things, or sob at what seems to be minor provocation. Because the situation has brought to mind some previous, traumatic experience to which they are responding, their reactions seem fully reasonable to them, but observers may notice that the response seems extreme for the situation.

Another frequent indicator that someone has been triggered is when they seem to respond to something that didn't actually happen. It's not uncommon for people who are triggered to say things like, "Stop comparing me to my mother!" or "I'll never be good enough!" when the person to whom they were speaking said nothing at all about their mother or about being good enough. However, for the person being triggered, whatever happened has reminded them of some other incident, and they are responding now to that earlier experience.

Many people feel caught off guard by own their behavior when they've been triggered. They may feel they were simply going about their lives when suddenly they found themselves sobbing for no reason, or screaming at a family member who is looking at them like they have two heads and saying, "But that's not what I said..." The person responded to a past situation without being aware of it at all, and this can be extremely disconcerting.

With practice, people can learn to recognize when they've been triggered by something in their environment. Often, the first step is to trust the people nearby who notice your behavior is a little off. If someone you trust is telling you that you're overreacting, or that you keep accusing them of doing things they haven't done, consider the possibility that they're right. There's no shame in being triggered – it's a biological act that ensured your and your ancestors' survival. But if people you trust tell that your behavior seems counterproductive, excessive, or that you keep responding to things that didn't even happen, you may want to begin to pay attention to how you feel and what happened to lead up to that moment.

In some ways, gifted individuals may have an easier time than neurotypical people in recognizing triggering experiences. Gifted people are frequently extremely good at pattern recognition, and identifying triggering is about understanding patterns of stimulus and response. You can begin to notice that you always seem to hear the same comments from friends and family, and you can begin to recognize that those people consistently deny that they said whatever you heard. You can learn to see the patterns in the behavior you seem to consistently receive from others, and you can begin to notice the times when you're upset about someone's behavior and they deny having done whatever upset you. You can begin to tune in to the times when your reactions are out of proportion to what's happening. The act of recognizing that we've been triggered is a big first step in pulling oneself out of the past and reacting instead to what is actually happening in front of us.

## EFT to Help

EFT can be used to address negative triggering situations in both the short and long terms. It can calm you down quickly so that you're no longer reacting to past events, and it can make it so those past events cease to be a problem. Note that because EFT does not affect and cannot remove positive emotions, it is the ideal solution for dealing with negative experiences without risk of unintentionally affecting positive memories.

In the short term, EFT can be used to curtail the experience of being in a negatively triggered state. Once we've been triggered, we're trapped in emotions from the past until the episode runs its course. However, when we use EFT to address our current condition, we can release the negative emotions that have flared up, ending the event and allowing us to feel better in the immediate term.

It's impossible for a script to walk through exactly what you or your loved ones feel when you've been triggered, but this one may get you started as you begin to release whatever emotions have been brought up by the situation. Feel free to continue to tap at any point along the script, adding whatever emotions or details seem appropriate to help you clear all the sensations that have emerged.

| Point | Statement |
| --- | --- |
| Karate chop | Even though I'm feeling triggered right now, I'm trying to accept how I feel and who I am.<br><br>Even though I'm feeling upset and {something} and I'm not even sure where they came from, I'm trying to treat myself with love and compassion.<br><br>Even though I'm really flooded with emotions right now that don't belong to this place and time, |

*Triggering*

| Point | Statement |
|---|---|
|  | I'm going to treat myself with kindness and love because I deserve it. |
| *Above the eye* | I'm feeling triggered. |
| *Side of the eye* | Something has set me off. |
| *Under the eye* | I may not know what it was… |
| *Under the nose* | But I know I'm kind of freaking out right now. |
| *Under the mouth* | I'm feeling *{something}* |
| *Collarbone* | And I'm feeling *{something else}* |
| *Under the arm* | And it feels very natural to feel this way right now |
| *Top of the head* | Because of *{what just happened}*. |
| *Above the eye* | It made me think of *{something}* |
| *Side of the eye* | And it upset me. |
| *Under the eye* | But no matter how natural and logical my response is, or seems to be, |
| *Under the nose* | I don't need to hold on to these emotions. |
| *Under the mouth* | I can choose to release the feelings that are coming up. |
| *Collarbone* | I can just let them go. |
| *Under the arm* | I can choose to remember that right now, I'm safe. |
| *Top of the head* | Whatever happened in the past is just a memory |
| *Above the eye* | And *{memory}* isn't happening right now. |
| *Side of the eye* | So I'm letting go of feeling *{something}* |
| *Under the eye* | And I'm releasing my feelings of *{something else}* |

55

| Point | Statement |
|---|---|
| Under the nose | I'm letting it all go. |
| Under the mouth | I'm letting all my tension and upset leave my body. |
| Collarbone | I'm taking deep, healing breaths. |
| Under the arm | I'm safe and okay. |
| Top of the head | And all shall be well. |
| Take a deep breath in through your nose... Hold it for a few seconds... Release it slowly through your mouth. | |

One of the most noteworthy long-term benefits of EFT is that it can help to eliminate the emotional suffering associated with past traumatic events. The emotions associated with those events can be processed and released once and for all, which will allow you to feel little or no distress when recalling those incidents in the future. In addition to removing that long-standing pain, using EFT to clear those events means they won't be triggered again. Current events won't call that particular trauma to mind anymore, so you'll be triggered less often going forward and will be able to experience whatever is happening in the present without interference from painful past memories.

EFT is by far one of the safest, most effective methods ever devised to clear the pain of old memories, but some caution is advised. We've *all* experienced some level of trauma, because we all have a "worst memory ever." While an objective observer might say that your worst memory seems like it would be much more painful than mine, each of those memories is, for each of us, the worst memories of our entire lives, and they hurt. Also, some of us have more traumatic memories than others due to our dispositions and life experiences.

It's virtually impossible for EFT itself to hurt anyone, but digging around in old trauma can be dangerous for some people, particularly individuals who have suffered severe emotional injuries. Sometimes even to remember a harrowing experience can cause someone to be re-traumatized, so while I'm going to include a script for clearing an old memory, please remember not to go where you don't belong. If you find that the memory being triggered is severely traumatic, or if you or your loved one has experienced severe or repeated traumatic events, please seek appropriate professional help before using EFT to clear those memories. While EFT can often offer relief from old traumatic pain in a way nothing else can, it may be best done with the support of a therapist, counselor, or EFT practitioner.

If the memory you're working to clear is not severely traumatic, you should be able to tap through it yourself. Remember that when using EFT to clear a memory, you want to work on a short, very specific incident, ideally one that lasted for no more than a moment or two. As you know, EFT works best with a narrow focus.

Also note that it's important to address all aspects of that memory, because anything you don't clear will continue to cause you distress. Tap through everything in the memory that stands out. Focus on each of your senses in turn, and also on what you thought at the time. For example, if you're trying to clear the memory of a time your brother hurt your feelings, you would want to tap through the words he said, the look on his face, where you were when it happened, even the thoughts that went through your head when he spoke. You want to get as many aspects as you can.

The point of tapping through the memory is not to relive the experience, but to process and heal it. Therefore, after you tap through the details, you should explicitly acknowledge and release the emotions surrounding the memory. You may want to be up front about choosing to leave behind anything that no longer serves you, so that any painful emotions are cleared away.

Tapping in this way should remove your distress when you recall the event going forward. The memory itself will remain, but the pain you feel should be reduced or even eliminated. As noted in Chapter Two, you can use the SUDs scale to measure your progress and can make note of physical indicators to judge whether you've cleared your emotional blocks about the event. You can also tap through the memory again if any negative emotions remain.

As mentioned before, it's impossible for a script in a book to walk through exactly what you or your loved ones experienced, but this should get you started as you begin to process and release the memories from your past. Feel free to continue to tap at any point along the script,

## Triggering

adding whatever details seem appropriate to help you clear the entire event.

One last reminder: permanently eliminating the pain associated with old memories is a wonderful, amazing benefit of EFT, but it can be physically and mentally taxing. As noted previously, you may experience some symptoms during and after the release of old feelings, and the more painful the incident was, and the longer you've been carrying those negative emotions, the more likely you are to feel some effects following your EFT session. Rest, stay hydrated, and be kind to yourself.

| Point | Statement |
| --- | --- |
| Karate chop | Even though I remember {this event}, I love and accept myself anyway. |
| | Even though I'm troubled by memories of {this event}, I love and forgive myself now. |
| | Even though I have these memories of {this incident}, and they still bother me after all this time, I choose to love, accept, and forgive myself, and maybe the other people involved. |
| Above the eye | I remember when {this event} happened. |
| Side of the eye | And even though I don't really want to think about it, |
| Under the eye | I'm going to face it now so that it will release its hold on me. |
| Under the nose | I remember where I was. |

| Point | Statement |
|---|---|
| Under the mouth | I was {in this place} |
| Collarbone | At {this time of day/ year} |
| Under the arm | And I was with {person}. NOTE: Keep tapping under the arm as you list everyone important in the scene. |
| Top of the head | I remember so many things about that moment. |
| Above the eye | I saw {this}. |
| Side of the eye | And I heard {this}. NOTE: Keep tapping through the points as you list as many specific details of the setting as you can. |
| Under the eye | And mostly I remember what happened. |
| Under the nose | {This happened}. |
| Under the mouth | And then {this happened}. NOTE: Keep tapping through the points as you list as many details of the event as you can. |
| Collarbone | And I felt {this}. NOTE: Keep tapping through the points, and be honest about how you felt in that moment. |
| Under the arm | And I thought {this}. NOTE: Keep tapping through the points as you honestly list what you thought at the time. |
| Top of the head | And I wish it had never happened! |
| Above the eye | At least I wish I could forget it all. |
| Side of the eye | Because it {hurt me/ scared me/ made me angry, etc}. |
| Under the eye | And it hasn't ever really gone away. |

| Point | Statement |
|---|---|
| Under the nose | I've waited for time to heal this wound |
| Under the mouth | But that hasn't happened. |
| Collarbone | And anyone who had been through {this event} would feel exactly as I do. |
| Under the arm | And anyone who had been through what I went through would still be bothered by it today. |
| Top of the head | My feelings are completely normal |
| Above the eye | And if I want to, I can feel this way for the rest of my life! |
| Side of the eye | But I don't want to. |
| Under the eye | I want it not to bother me anymore. |
| Under the nose | I'd like to let my {pain/ fear/ anger, etc} go. |
| Under the mouth | I'm not sure I can do that. |
| Collarbone | I've been carrying this {pain/ fear/ anger, etc} for a long time. |
| Under the arm | But I'm going to try to let it go now. |
| Top of the head | I'm ready to release my {pain/ fear/ anger, etc}. |
| Above the eye | I'm willing to release my {pain/ fear/ anger, etc}. |
| Side of the eye | I'm choosing to release my {pain/ fear/ anger, etc}. |
| Under the eye | I'm choosing to let it all go. |
| Under the nose | I'm also choosing to release any shame I felt at the time |
| Under the mouth | And any shame I feel about {this event} today. |

| Point | Statement |
|---|---|
| Collarbone | I forgive myself for anything I did wrong, or think I did wrong, |
| Under the arm | Because I did the best I could at the time |
| Top of the head | And I treat myself with kindness and compassion. |
| Above the eye | And now I'm releasing any remaining {pain/ fear/ anger, etc}. |
| Side of the eye | I'm releasing them from every fiber of my being |
| Under the eye | And all the way back through my past. |
| Under the nose | I know that my memories will remain |
| Under the mouth | But the painful emotions can go now. |
| Collarbone | I'm ready to move forward without them. |
| Under the arm | I'm setting myself free from my old pain |
| Top of the head | Because I deserve to be at peace. |
| *Take a deep breath in through your nose...* *Hold it for a few seconds...* *Release it slowly through your mouth.* | |

PART TWO

# Academic Challenges

Although academic prowess is the usual way gifted children are identified, giftedness doesn't preclude the existence of academic challenges. Sometimes, learning faster than nearly everyone else in one's class can have serious downsides.

*Tapping for the Gifted Child*

CHAPTER FOUR

# Boredom

In the life of the parent of every gifted child is something that, for lack of a better term, is called "The 'Oh, Crap!' Moment." It's the moment when the parent recognizes that the child they've been given isn't quite what they were expecting, and life isn't going to play out in the way they had anticipated. It's the moment when they begin to see that their child's giftedness makes them different in tangible ways from other children, and they begin to have an inkling of what that may mean. For many parents, this moment arrives when they realize that their child, who has "no good reason" to be bored in school, is bored anyway.

For Joy's parents, that moment came when their six-year-old daughter flat-out refused to get on the school bus. "I'm not going," she insisted. "I don't learn anything there. It's a waste of my time."

Her parents had assured her from the very first day that the pace of learning would accelerate over time. Now, six weeks into the school year, when her fellow first-graders were *still* learning to read, Joy was having none of it. Her mother believed that Joy had the right to stand up for herself but felt something akin to panic. She had no idea what to do in this situation. None of the parenting books she had read dealt with this at all.

Joy's *need* to learn, so common among gifted students, wasn't being met in her traditional classroom. Unfortunately, in traditional classrooms, boredom is so common as to be almost synonymous with giftedness. It can cause strife between parents and children, tension between home and school, and leads to a wide variety of negative outcomes for children, with repercussions that can last a lifetime.

In the United States, children spend roughly six hours per day in school, for an average of 180 days per year, for thirteen consecutive years. That's a total of 14,040 hours spent in the classroom over the course of a K-12 education.

Sadly, schools weren't generally created for people who master material quickly and need little to no repetition in order to retain that material. Most schools teach to the mythical "average" student, and students who have the ability to learn at a faster pace find themselves bored with the slow speed of the introduction of new material. Many students also need at least some repetition of material in class in order to master and retain that material, yet gifted students may not require that repetition, leading to yet more boredom. And often, homework assignments are designed to assist students with comprehending and remembering material that the gifted student may have mastered on the initial hearing, or may have even known before it was introduced in class. The typical school setting leaves a lot of time for students to feel bored and frustrated.

> Repetition is a part of learning, parents and educators agree, but research shows gifted children need far less repetition than most students. ...
>
> The gifted child realizes quickly that B follows A, or even further, that C, D, and E come quickly after. He understands inherently why this is, how each step works, and he wants, and needs to continue his progress. But the teacher must gear instruction to 95% of the children in her class...This is not progress for a gifted child, it is torture.
>
> Worse, the gifted child often comes into the grade knowing 80% or more of the school year's material. For the gifted child, it's not a matter of repetition of what you're learning. It's a matter of repetition of what you knew when you walked in the classroom door on the first day of school. (Kottmeyer, 2008)

Moreover, the more gifted the student, the more likely he or she is to find school less challenging than he or she hoped it would be. Gifted students sometimes ask for more rigorous work or for the chance to move ahead in subjects that interest them, yet schools are often reluctant to advance students based on ability rather than age, which can lead to further frustration.

Parents should remain alert to the possibility that lack of challenge in school may lead to psychological triggering of children's previous experiences with boredom. When children are prevented from moving at their desired pace, they may be subconsciously reminded of earlier times when they felt frustrated by the pace or material in the classroom, and this may prevent them from accurately perceiving what is happening in the present.

## What It Looks Like

Adults frequently equate boredom with lack of engagement. When bored, they may daydream, stare at a clock, or look around the room or out the window. Children will often exhibit these same behaviors when bored in class; however, when boredom continues day after day, lack of engagement will often morph into anger. "Bored, for a gifted child, is better described as frustration with the lack of progress" (Kottmeyer, 2008). Students may become overtly angry, may act negatively, or may be rude in class.

For many gifted students, boredom ultimately becomes despondency. They may lose hope that things will ever get better, or they may feel that something is wrong with them because they alone seem to be suffering in school. They may become depressed or self-critical. Older students may drop out of school, and some may even become suicidal when they can't bear to remain in school despite pressure and expectations to graduate.

*Putting students with exceptional academic abilities in classrooms where their talents are constrained, rather than*

> nurtured, is the first step toward courting trouble, experts say. The rule of thumb tends to be the more gifted a child, the greater the disparity between a student's ability and age and the greater the risk for emotional and social problems.
>
> Depression. Delinquency. Dropping out. And even suicide. Gifted children, who some say are smart enough to know better, are not immune to such dangers. (Malone, 2004)

## Strategies to Consider

Unless you address the underlying lack of challenge, your child will continue to experience boredom in school, because the only real solution to boredom is to provide appropriate intellectual stimulation and challenge to the child.

There are a number of ways to do this: through subject matter acceleration, grade skips, pull-out programs, after schooling, dual enrollment, early college, or homeschooling. There are many resources available to support parents as they work to provide appropriate challenges for their children, and some of these are listed in the Resources section at the end of the book, but this list is by no means comprehensive.

Don't forget to look locally for possible resources. Your school district may be able to suggest local programs for budding scientists or may offer classes that are only available to residents. Nearby museums, libraries, or parks may offer courses or enrichment activities that engage your child. Many community organizations are open to anyone, regardless of age, and many young photographers, astronomers, and painters have found mentors in local clubs. If you have a college or university near your home, you have access to many potential tutors and mentors who can work with your child on his or her areas of interest.

The internet provides a wealth of resources for gifted children. You can find individual classes in any subject imaginable and can also find online schools that offer a complete online education. Many students particularly enjoy online classes because they're often able to work at their intellectual level rather than their age; teachers and other students often don't have any way of gauging one another's age and simply interact based on what happens in the classroom.

## EFT to Help

EFT cannot, by itself, eliminate your child's boredom in school; structural changes of some sort will probably be required to make your child's educational environment a better fit. Unfortunately, for a variety of reasons, not all gifted students are in a position to have their needs for intellectual challenge met, or the timing of the structural changes to the child's life may not be fast enough to suit the child. In these cases, EFT can be used to relieve some of the suffering boredom causes.

Below is a tapping routine that may alleviate the frustration that so often accompanies boredom. Remember, as you lead your child through the script, you should feel free to continue to tap at any point along the

*Boredom*

script, adding whatever details seem appropriate to help your child clear the aggravation he or she feels.

| Point | Statement |
|---|---|
| Karate chop | Even though I'm frustrated because of how slowly things move in school, I accept how I feel and who I am.<br><br>Even though I'm angry because I just go to school and waste so much time every day, I love and accept myself anyway.<br><br>Even though I'm really angry because I don't get to learn what I want, when I want, I deeply and completely love, accept, and forgive myself. |
| Above the eye | I'm angry. |
| Side of the eye | I'm so ANGRY! |
| Under the eye | School is a waste of time. |
| Under the nose | All they do is tell us things I already know. |
| Under the mouth | And then they repeat it again and again. |
| Collarbone | I'm bored all the time! |
| Under the arm | I want to do things that are interesting. |
| Top of the head | I want and need to learn something new! |
| Above the eye | And I get so mad when they won't let me. |
| Side of the eye | I feel like I don't matter when my needs are ignored all the time. |
| Under the eye | I'm hurt and frustrated and bored. |

| Point | Statement |
|---|---|
| Under the nose | And that's okay. |
| Under the mouth | Anyone would feel this way if they had to spend all day bored every day. |
| Collarbone | It's okay for me to feel angry. |
| Under the arm | But it's probably not okay for me to {act out} the way I have been. |
| Top of the head | Because then people see my behavior and not my boredom... |
| Above the eye | And things will never get better if they think I'm just a pain. |
| Side of the eye | I need to be able to explain what I need. |
| Under the eye | And I need to remember that school does end. |
| Under the nose | I will be able to live an interesting life once I'm done with school. |
| Under the mouth | This isn't all there is. |
| Collarbone | I'm open to finding new ways to keep myself engaged while I'm at school. |
| Under the arm | And I'm choosing to know things will get better. |
| Top of the head | Things will get better in time. |
| Take a deep breath in through your nose... Hold it for a few seconds... Release it slowly through your mouth. | |

Also remember that if triggering of previous traumatic experiences with poor academic fit is taking place, using the tools for addressing triggering may defuse the situation somewhat. Both addressing the negative emotions that have surfaced in the immediate term, and going back and clearing the pain of earlier events, can free children from feeling overwhelmed by seemingly continuous experiences of boredom. This may reduce the feeling that school is one long, continuous experience of tedium and misunderstanding, and students' suffering should be significantly reduced. See Chapter Three for details.

CHAPTER FIVE

# Imposter Syndrome

Destiny's father sighed into the telephone, unsure what to say to his daughter as she scrolled frantically through the website, looking for the link to the Withdrawal form. Although she was slated to begin graduate school in the morning, she had called in a panic, desperate to find a way to cancel her enrollment.

She'd always been a straight-A student, and he'd been so proud when she graduated from both high school and college with honors. Her advisors had written glowing letters of recommendation when she applied for this PhD program, but Destiny had been surprised when she was admitted. It was a highly competitive program, and she said there had to have been many applicants more qualified than she was.

Even so, she had been excited to attend, and her dad had been happy to help her move across the country. This morning, however, she'd called from her new apartment, afraid to begin classes. She said she would be surrounded by brilliant people who deserved this opportunity. What if they recognized that she wasn't able to do work of the same caliber they did? What if the school realized its mistake in admitting her, and publicly asked her to leave?

Her father knew he couldn't let her sabotage her participation in her PhD program, but he had no idea what to say to his daughter. Despite years of evidence that she is an extremely capable student, Destiny continually discounted her many successes. Telling her that she'd be fine had made no difference at all, nor had it helped to point out that probably *everyone* in the program was nervous today. What was he supposed to do now?

Imposter syndrome is a feeling that one is a fraud, accompanied by an ongoing fear that someone else may learn the truth about one's abilities and expose the fraud to the world. In a school setting, imposter syndrome commonly manifests as a belief that one is stupid, and commonly develops among children who are not working at a level commensurate with their abilities. Imposter syndrome afflicts both boys and girls, but some scientists believe it is more common among girls. (Kanazawa & Perina, 2009)

For people who do not have imposter syndrome, the entire problem seems counterintuitive. How can someone who learns quickly and retains information easily possibly think that he or she is stupid?

One common way that imposter syndrome develops goes like this: A gifted child who is engaged with the material will often have questions that go far beyond the standard lesson – *how* does this happen, *why* does it happen, what does it mean when it *doesn't* happen? Sometimes the teacher will answer all these questions gladly, but there are times when he or she may not know the answer, or may have other lessons to get to, and displays impatience with the gifted student's questions. The gifted student begins to learn that there is something wrong with his or her questions and the way in which he or she learns.

In some cases, the gifted student may begin to recognize that he or she is frequently the only student who has questions for the teacher at all. The lesson as planned may satisfy the needs of neurotypical children, but it may not go into enough detail to satisfy children whose minds are trying to learn more, to build unusual connections, or to understand deeper meanings. However, the gifted child may not recognize that all the questions he or she has are a result of his or her desire to know more, and instead may feel these questions indicate a failure of understanding. He or she may begin to feel less capable than his or her classmates.

Sometimes, the gifted student may finish a test quickly and find all the questions easy. However, when he or she discusses the test afterwards with classmates, some students may have found the test challenging. "Wasn't that hard?" may be the common refrain, but the gifted student didn't find it so. "What's wrong with me?" he or she may wonder. "Why am I so stupid that I don't even understand why the test was hard?"

And then comes the day when someone – most commonly a teacher, but possibly a parent, neighbor, or relative – will make an offhand remark about how some material being covered is easy for the gifted student, and the student will think, "No, it's not easy for me! I'm so stupid I don't even understand why I'm stupid! If you knew me better, you'd know how stupid I really am!" This thought reveals the existence of full-blown imposter syndrome: a belief that one is less capable than one's fellows, and a fear that if only other people "knew the truth," the student would be revealed to be less competent than others.

Cognitive dissonance is the name for the mental stress that arises from trying to hold two contradictory ideas simultaneously, and it plays a crucial role in the life of a person with imposter syndrome. The child *feels* that he or she is less capable than others, yet evidence such as grades will frequently point to the idea that the student is *more* capable than classmates. Thus, in order to avoid the discomforts of cognitive dissonance, once a skewed image of oneself has been established, the student will go to great lengths to explain away the successes that run counter to his or her self-perceptions. Luck, favoritism, and other mysterious forces are given credit for successful, even superior, performance. The student will find him or herself unable to take credit for work well done because that runs counter to his or her self-image as a poor performer who is "slipping by."

For this reason, the syndrome doesn't dissipate when the child performs well over time, and in fact may become more debilitating. The student can't see his or her abilities objectively, so each success is seen as another fluke that only reinforces the belief that more and more people have "fallen for" the idea that the student is capable. The risk of discovery becomes more terrifying with each achievement because the student believes he or she has deceived ever-increasing numbers of people.

## What It Looks Like

Children with imposter syndrome generally do well in school, which may lull parents into thinking there isn't a problem. However, when they do well on a test or project, these students will frequently say things like, "The teacher likes me," "I got lucky," or, "Mr. Smith is an easy grader." They frequently find it impossible to accept praise for their accomplishments.

Students may also spend inordinate amounts of time on their homework or studying for tests, afraid that if they aren't perfect in their work, they will be found out as frauds.

## Strategies to Consider

Imposter syndrome can set children up for a lifetime of anxiety and low self-esteem. Feeling that you're not as good as the people around you can be depressing, and living in constant fear of discovery can be exhausting.

Sometimes people believe that giving a person with imposter syndrome challenges equal to his or her abilities will alleviate the problem, but that is rarely successful for people with imposter syndrome as it is for students who are bored. The student with imposter syndrome has learned to attribute success to factors other than his or her abilities and will likely continue to attribute any success with more difficult material to those same outside factors, simply continuing the situation.

Rather than adjusting the environment, disarming imposter syndrome requires that parents and professionals address the skewed perception of self which is the basis of the disorder. To this end, it can sometimes be helpful to discuss the situation directly. It can be extremely reassuring to a child to hear that asking frequent questions is a sign of deeper, rather than lesser, understanding. The student may be reassured to know that he or she can follow lines of inquiry outside the classroom and learn independently without needing to "annoy the teacher" with constant questions. Students may be relieved to know that tests that seem easy to them may, in fact, be easy for them, no matter how the questions are perceived by classmates. And students are often comforted to hear that the ways in which they learn may differ from the students around them, but these are perfectly valid ways to learn and that there is nothing wrong with them.

## EFT to Help

Unfortunately, thousands of people who have been in therapy can attest that simply hearing the truth about themselves and their situations doesn't necessarily alleviate their problems. Many people are able to say the "right" things about themselves without truly *believing* those things, and this is where EFT can be of assistance.

EFT can help people move from "knowing" something is true in their heads, to actually "feeling" that it's true in their hearts. It can therefore be a valuable adjunct to explanations in addressing imposter syndrome.

Note that even using EFT may not result in a quick change to a long-held self-perception, no matter how inaccurate that self-perception may appear to the outsider. It may take numerous sessions of EFT to help the student move from a firmly held belief that one is a fraud to an equally firmly held belief that one is capable. Patience and persistence may well be required.

Initially, EFT can be used to lessen the hold of the old self-perception and to establish the possibility of seeing oneself differently. Subsequent sessions can be used to move the student in the direction of believing in one's abilities.

| Point | Statement |
| --- | --- |
| Karate chop | Even though I feel like I'm not as {good/smart/etc} as the other kids in my class, I'm trying to accept myself just as I am.<br><br>Even though I feel like everyone else is smarter than I am, I love and accept myself anyway.<br><br>Even though I feel like I only do well because {I'm lucky/ my teacher likes me/ etc}, I completely love, accept, and forgive myself. |
| Above the eye | I feel like a fraud. |

## Imposter Syndrome

| Point | Statement |
|---|---|
| Side of the eye | I feel like I'm not as capable as the other kids in my class. |
| Under the eye | And I'm afraid someone will find out. |
| Under the nose | I'm afraid they will tell everyone that I'm a fake. |
| Under the mouth | And then I'll be an outcast. No one will {like me/ respect me / be my friend}. |
| Collarbone | I'm constantly afraid of being found out. |
| Under the arm | And I hear what {someone} is saying, that maybe I'm not as big a fake as I feel like. |
| Top of the head | But it sure doesn't feel that way from here. |
| Above the eye | I've felt like a fraud every day for years, and I'm so scared of having people learn the truth about me. |
| Side of the eye | I'm tired, too. |
| Under the eye | It's exhausting having to pretend all the time to be something that I'm not. |
| Under the nose | I wish I could be myself. |
| Under the mouth | Mostly, I wish the real me were as good as people think {he/she} is. |
| Collarbone | But since I'm not, I have to go on pretending to be better than I am, and hope that no one figures out the truth. |
| Under the arm | But what if it's possible – just possible! – that {someone} is right? |
| Top of the head | What if it were possible that I really am smart? |

| Point | Statement |
|---|---|
| Above the eye | What if it were possible that I really can do well at school, not because *(I'm lucky/ my teacher likes me, etc)* but because I'm pretty capable? |
| Side of the eye | What if the way I've learned to see myself is wrong? |
| Under the eye | I don't know if I can handle that! It's hard to even imagine! |
| Under the nose | I've known for so long that I'm not as good as the other kids! |
| Under the mouth | It doesn't seem possible that I've been wrong for so long. |
| Collarbone | But I'm going to choose now to open myself to the possibility that the way I see myself may be wrong. |
| Under the arm | It's possible that I'm smart, maybe even very smart. |
| Top of the head | It's possible that I'm good at school. |
| Above the eye | It's possible that I'm good at many things. |
| Side of the eye | I don't have to believe it all today. |
| Under the eye | But starting now, I'm going to be open to the idea that I'm good at what I do. |
| Under the nose | I'm going to be open to the idea that I have amazing gifts and abilities, |
| Under the mouth | And those gifts and abilities are responsible for my success. |

| Point | Statement |
|---|---|
| Collarbone | It's NOT because {my teacher likes me/ I got lucky, etc} |
| Under the arm | Maybe, just maybe, my success is due to what I do. |
| Top of the head | I'm not sure I buy it, but I'm going to keep an open mind. |
| Take a deep breath in through your nose... Hold it for a few seconds... Release it slowly through your mouth. | |

Once the student has internalized the idea that his or her self-perception may not be accurate, subsequent sessions can be used to move the student in the direction of believing in one's abilities.

| Point | Statement |
|---|---|
| Karate chop | Even though it feels strange to think that I may be {good/smart/etc}, I want to accept myself just as I am.<br><br>Even though I've felt like a fake for a long time and it seems impossible that I'm not, I love, accept, and forgive myself anyway.<br><br>Even though I'm really not sure I'm as capable as people seem to think I am, I am trying to |

*Tapping for the Gifted Child*

| Point | Statement |
|---|---|
|  | deeply and completely love, accept, and forgive myself. |
| *Above the eye* | There are a lot of people who seem to think I'm pretty {smart/ capable/ good at ___}. |
| *Side of the eye* | {Someone} thinks so. |
| *Under the eye* | {Someone else} thinks so. |
| *Under the nose* | It's hard for me to think so, because I'm not used to thinking that way. |
| *Under the mouth* | But what if those people are right? |
| *Collarbone* | I generally trust those people. |
| *Under the arm* | They seem pretty reliable. |
| *Top of the head* | Now that I think about it, maybe they're not all that easy to fool. |
| *Above the eye* | Maybe I'm not fooling anyone. |
| *Side of the eye* | Maybe they're able to see what I can do. |
| *Under the eye* | Maybe they're RIGHT about what I can do! |
| *Under the nose* | Wouldn't that be something? What if they're right about me? |
| *Under the mouth* | What if I am as *{smart/ capable/ good, etc}* as they think I am? |
| *Collarbone* | That would be pretty cool! |
| *Under the arm* | And maybe the reason I feel different from the other kids in my class is because I AM different from the other kids in my class. |
| *Top of the head* | Not less *{smart/ capable, etc}* but just different. |

*Imposter Syndrome*

| Point | Statement |
|---|---|
| *Above the eye* | Being different doesn't mean something bad. |
| *Side of the eye* | Maybe in this case, it's something good. |
| *Under the eye* | Maybe I really AM *{smart/ capable, etc}* |
| *Under the nose* | And maybe my success really is due to my abilities. |
| *Under the mouth* | I'm going to try to believe this for a while. |
| *Collarbone* | If it seems that it's not true, I can always go back to believing that I'm fooling people. |
| *Under the arm* | But for now, I choose to believe that I am NOT a fraud. |
| *Top of the head* | I choose to see myself as a capable person. |
| *Above the eye* | I choose to know that no one is going to expose me as a fake. |
| *Side of the eye* | It's okay for me to relax and let my guard down. |
| *Under the eye* | It's safe for me to think of myself as a capable, successful person. |
| *Under the nose* | It's okay for me to remember that I'm not just pretending to do well. |
| *Under the mouth* | I really DO do well. |
| *Collarbone* | And now I'm willing to think of myself as a capable, successful person, |
| *Under the arm* | Because I AM a successful person, who does many things well. |
| *Top of the head* | I am a successful person, who does many things well. |

| Point | Statement |
|---|---|
| *Take a deep breath in through your nose...* | |
| *Hold it for a few seconds...* | |
| *Release it slowly through your mouth.* | |

CHAPTER SIX

# Twice Exceptionality

Mikey's mother tried to control her frustration, but it wasn't easy. His report card was full of C's again! What was going on?

Mikey's older brother did well in school. He got straight A's, did his work, and didn't complain, but Mikey *hated* school. He didn't do poorly, exactly, but he didn't do well. He didn't enjoy books and considered reading to be difficult and boring. He struggled with his homework and rarely completed his assignments. The only reason he wasn't failing his classes was because he aced every test he took. He complained about school constantly and often wished aloud that he didn't have a brother, because then no one would criticize his grades.

His mother knew Mikey was a bright kid, but she was frustrated by his poor school performance and irritated by the fact that he spent all his free time building with blocks. Her father, a carpenter, saved wood scraps for his grandson, giving Mikey a large and diverse collection of building materials. Beginning when he was a toddler, he would create elaborate, enormous block buildings, four feet on a side. He would eagerly show his mother his creations, removing walls to reveal secret passages and hidden rooms, and then he would say, "And if I take out this block *right here*... the whole things will come down." Inevitably, he was right. He was a genius with blocks. He clearly had ability. Why wasn't he doing better in school?

A common misperception about gifted individuals is that they learn everything equally easily, but nothing could be further from the truth. Although there are a great many globally gifted individuals in the world, most gifted individuals excel in some areas more than in others. There are "words kids" and "math kids" and musical geniuses; most gifted people have areas of specialization that simply come more easily than others.

The areas where these individuals perform less well vary widely. For many gifted people, especially highly gifted individuals, their overall performance is so high that their performance in weaker areas is still considered "gifted" or at least "normal" by objective standards, and only seems inferior when compared to their areas of strength. However, there are many gifted children whose performance in their area of weakness truly lags behind the typical performance that would be expected of people of their age. In fact, many people who are identified as gifted also have learning disabilities.

This seems counterintuitive, even impossible, to many people. It seems unlikely that a student who is generally able to learn quickly and easily retain information would have one or two subjects where he or she is working at a remedial level, yet this is surprisingly common. The brains of many gifted people are simply wired differently from the brains of neurotypical individuals, and many of the same neural changes within the brain that confer gifts in some areas also confer challenges in others.

The existence of a student who is simultaneously gifted and learning disabled is so common that it has its own name: twice exceptional, or 2E. These are the children whose work is far ahead of their peers in some areas and far behind their peers in others, and thus they are exceptional in two very different ways.

It is impossible to make definitive statements about learning disabilities within the gifted population because of the variety in individual situations. Individuals may have one disability or many, and their challenges may take many forms. There are strictly academic challenges, such as dyslexia, dyscalculia, and dysgraphia; there are more global issues with attention and focus, such as attention deficit disorder, attention deficit hyperactivity disorder, and obsessive compulsive disorder. There may be issues with working memory or processing speed. There are difficulties handling sensory input, such as sensory processing disorder, as well as more specific issues with visual or auditory processing. Gifted individuals can also experience all forms of mental and physical illness, and while these may not technically be learning disabilities, mental and physical illness can certainly affect a student's ability to perform effectively in educational settings. Some studies even indicate that gifted people are more sensitive to their environments than neurotypical individuals, and thus may experience more food and environmental allergies than the general population, which can also affect academic success. The challenges facing gifted students can be plentiful and profound.

Moreover, these challenges are often stubbornly resistant to remediation. The very nature of learning disabilities indicates that these are weaknesses beyond your typical academic struggles. Consistent, applied study in the area of weakness may provide no apparent improvement at all, or, more maddening for children, parents, and teachers alike, may *seem* to provide improvement or even breakthroughs one day, only to have those gains seep away seemingly overnight. The inability to learn or retain information, frustrating though it is, truly isn't the student's fault. Many learning disabilities have their roots in neurological changes in brain structure or function from "normal" brains. There are children – gifted and not – who are simply not wired to easily master some material.

For children who are accustomed to learning easily and quickly, having ongoing, sometimes inexplicable, failure in one or more areas can lead them to feel shame, grief, or rage, and because learning disabilities are often unrecognized in gifted individuals, parents and teachers may inadvertently exacerbate the situation. The child may be accused of being lazy, of not trying hard enough, or of not caring about his or her work, because it may seem impossible that a child so capable could honestly struggle so much with some material. The emotional injuries from failure, particularly repeated, inexplicable failure, can be deep and long lasting; the injuries from being unfairly accused of being lazy or uncaring can be as bad or worse, especially for the many gifted children who are deeply concerned with fairness. Undiagnosed or unremediated learning disabilities can cause grave and ongoing suffering for gifted children and those who care about them.

Additionally, many children with learning disabilities – gifted or not – often experience psychological triggering when dealing with their weaker areas. Particularly if there have been fights or shaming experiences with important adults in their lives in the past, any failures they experience in their area of weakness may immediately call to mind previous struggles with the same material, making it difficult for the child to see what is happening in the present. He or she may be trapped in memories of failure and may find it extremely difficult to put these experiences in context, because the parade of disappointments in this area is honestly all the child can see when in the throes of the triggering episode.

## What It Looks Like

Given the wide variety of disabilities and challenges that can affect gifted learners, it can be almost impossible to generalize about what it looks like to have a 2E child in your home.

However, one common indicator parents should be aware of is the existence of wide discrepancies between a student's abilities in some areas compared to others. Although it is certainly possible for students to have an area or two where his or her abilities are simply wildly stronger than others without disabilities being involved, as a general rule, wide discrepancies in ability signal that there's something amiss frequently enough that the situation may warrant further investigation.

Bear in mind that parents and teachers may find this discrepancy in abilities hard to see. Many gifted children are working at such a high level across the board that even though their work in their areas of weakness falls far below their work in their areas of strength, it may only fall to about the level of their classmates. Grades may show acceptable performance in all subjects. However, parents may note that homework in one subject may take a great deal more time than homework in another subject, or it may even take more time than the homework from all other subjects combined. Students may complain about certain subjects more than others, or they may avoid participating in optional activities that would require the student to use areas of weakness. Pronounced weakness in some areas will commonly drive students to focus more overtly on areas of strength.

Another common indication that something may require further review is reluctance to go to school. Many gifted individuals learn instinctively and even voraciously, and reluctance to attend an institution of learning generally signals that something isn't working for the student. The situation at issue may be anything from a need for eyeglasses to bullying to poor fit in the classroom, but parents should heed and investigate students' clear signals that something is not right.

Other indicators that parents may wish to watch for are emotional outbursts, particularly when talking about school. It is common for 2E students to feel stupid when they are unable to master material that other students quickly grasp, particularly when they are accustomed to learning many things easily. Many students in this situation will lash out in anger, while others may exhibit symptoms of depression. Students who are not used to struggling in school will frequently become very disconcerted when forced to confront inordinately challenging material.

Students with various disabilities may express a great deal of fear, some of which may seem out of proportion to the situation. They may feel afraid that they will never master certain material, that they'll flunk out of school, or even that they'll starve to death because they won't be able to get a job. Gifted children tend to be good at seeing patterns and drawing logical conclusions from relatively little data, but this trait may mean that the child only ends up frightening him- or herself at this moment. Also remember that gifted kids are often able to understand situations intellectually that they can't handle emotionally, and these exaggerated fears over poor performance may reflect that discrepancy. Parents and teachers will have to work with children to reassure them that they'll be okay in the long run.

Another indicator of possible 2E issues that parents and teachers may notice is that students who performed well in previous years begin to fall behind, often markedly, as they progress through school. Gifted students are frequently able to compensate for their disabilities by using their amazing abilities, and the more gifted the child, the better he or she may be at hiding weaknesses; however, as school work becomes more challenging, the student's compensation strategies cease to be effective.

For example, gifted children with dyslexia often possess advanced vocabularies and strong verbal language abilities, which may allow them to correctly guess at words they cannot read in a passage. As material becomes more advanced, however, their ability to guess at what has been written may not be close enough to understand the content and they may begin to perform poorly on reading-related activities. Although the ability to compensate for weakness by using their strengths is an advantage to these students, gifted children's tendencies to mask their weaknesses can make it challenging to understand why they suddenly begin to struggle in later years.

Remember, too, that whatever we grow up with is what we consider "normal," so it may not occur to your children to mention that they see double on the page or that they can't quite hear the teacher's words. You may have to be persistent in figuring out where your children's weaknesses lie and what compensation and remediation strategies may be effective in helping them succeed despite their challenges.

## Strategies to Consider

As with all the academic issues faced by gifted children, tapping alone won't solve students' problems. Depending on the disability they possess, students may need to learn compensation strategies to work around their deficits, and/or they may need to undertake remediation to bolster areas of weakness. Learning disabilities can be challenging to overcome, but strides can generally be made to reduce the impact of the disability on the student's life and performance.

## EFT to Help

Given the wide variety of situations facing 2E students as well as the neurological basis for many 2E challenges, it may seem that EFT can offer little benefit to 2E kids, but that's not the case. It's true that the sample tapping routines in this book may be too general to benefit some individuals, but the Emotional Freedom Techniques can be of supreme benefit to students who suffer from various disabilities. EFT can help students remain calm in the face of stress and fear, to release negative emotions associated with failure or teasing, and to put their relative abilities into perspective so that they can maintain a positive self-image in spite of their challenges. EFT is a valuable mechanism to support students emotionally as they face other work.

Remember that if triggering is involved, it will be beneficial to use EFT to address any negative emotions that have been brought to the surface, and it will likely be valuable to go back at a later time and address the painful memories that were triggered by the current situation. See Chapter Three for details.

Below is a sample tapping routine that can be used to address the negative emotions that may arise from having an area of weakness that is largely outside of their control. As mentioned before, it's impossible for a script in a book to cover exactly what you or your loved ones are going through, but this should allow you to acknowledge and begin releasing that negativity. As always, feel free to continue to tap at any point along the script, adding whatever details seem appropriate to help you clear the entire experience.

| Point | Statement |
|---|---|
| *Karate chop* | Even though I really struggle in *{math/ English/ other subject}*, I accept myself just as I am. |
| | Even though I've had problems in *{math/ English/ other subject}* for a long time now, I love, accept, and forgive myself. |
| | Even though I can't seem to do as well in *{math/ English/ other subject}* as I'd like, and it's *{frustrating/ scary/ irritating}*, I deeply and completely love and accept myself. |
| *Above the eye* | I struggle in *{math/ English/ other subject}*. |
| *Side of the eye* | Sometimes it feels like my struggles in *{math/ English/ other subject}* dominate my school day. |
| *Under the eye* | I try so hard to do well. |

| Point | Statement |
|---|---|
| Under the nose | I work so hard. |
| Under the mouth | And still I don't do as well as I want to. |
| Collarbone | I still feel like a failure. |
| Under the arm | I feel stupid. |
| Top of the head | Sometimes it feels like I'm the only person who can't do {math/ English/ other subject}. |
| Above the eye | It seems like it's easier for all the other kids than it is for me. |
| Side of the eye | Sometimes I worry that {I'll be held back/ I'll flunk out of school/ I'll never get a job} because I can't do {math/ English/ other subject} |
| Under the eye | And that's really scary. |
| Under the nose | But school is a weird place, when you think about it. |
| Under the mouth | In school, everyone has to be good at everything. |
| Collarbone | But real life isn't like that. |
| Under the arm | Once people are out of school, they don't have to be good at everything. |
| Top of the head | They're allowed to have strengths and weaknesses. |
| Above the eye | And once I'm done with school, I'll be allowed to have strengths and weaknesses. |
| Side of the eye | I won't be expected to be equally good at everything. |

| Point | Statement |
|---|---|
| Under the eye | It won't matter so much that I'm not all that good at {math/ English/ other subject}. |
| Under the nose | I'll be allowed to do things I'm good at and that I enjoy |
| Under the mouth | {Math/ English/ other subject} will be something I use less often. |
| Collarbone | And there are plenty of things I'm good at and enjoy doing. |
| Under the arm | I enjoy {something}. |
| Top of the head | And I'm good at {something else}. |
| Above the eye | And I'm also good {this other thing}. |
| Side of the eye | And I have lots of other good qualities, like I'm {funny/ thoughtful/ kind/ etc}. |
| Under the eye | I'm actually a pretty great person |
| Under the nose | And {math/ English/ other subject} is only a small part of my life. |
| Under the mouth | I'm not going to let it dominate how I see myself. |
| Collarbone | There's a lot more to me than being bad at {math/ English/ other subject}! |
| Under the arm | I'm not going to let the things I'm not good at be more important than the things I AM good at. |
| Top of the head | And I'm going to let my {frustration/ fear/ irritation} go. |
| Above the eye | It's possible that I'll get better at {math/ English/ other subject} over time |

| Point | Statement |
|---|---|
| *Side of the eye* | But even if I don't, I'm going to be okay. |
| *Under the eye* | I'm capable and smart and a good person. |
| *Under the nose* | And I have a great future ahead of me. |
| *Under the mouth* | I'm good enough just the way I am. |
| *Collarbone* | I don't have to be perfect in all things. |
| *Under the arm* | I accept myself fully, just as I am |
| *Top of the head* | Because I deserve it. |
| *Take a deep breath in through your nose...* *Hold it for a few seconds...* *Release it slowly through your mouth.* ||

*Tapping for the Gifted Child*

PART THREE

# Emotional Challenges

Although many people view giftedness as strictly an academic issue, giftedness actually affects all areas of life. Gifted individuals see the world differently from neurotypical individuals, and they may experience a wide range of emotional effects as a result of their abilities and differences.

*Tapping for the Gifted Child*

CHAPTER SEVEN

# Perfectionism

Lily's parents watched her release a torrent of angry tears, helpless to do anything to make her feel better. This time, the crisis was precipitated by the fact that her homework had taken all weekend, and she hadn't had time to write the extra credit paper for her English class. She *wanted* and *needed* to do that paper, despite the fact that she already had an A in English. It just wasn't in her to not turn in extra credit work.

Lily had always been this way – needing to do more than anyone else, needing to finish things perfectly, and becoming extremely upset if she fell short of her own incredibly high expectations at any point. She had sobbed her way furiously through learning to tie her shoes and ride a bicycle, and years later, her parents still shuddered slightly when they looked back on her piano lessons. She had never been able to tolerate needing to practice a new skill, always wanting to do things perfectly right away.

Lily seemed to be a highly successful young teen; she had high grades, lots of scout badges, and awards and prizes from all sorts of competitions. But Lily lived in a stressful world, constantly pressuring herself to do more and be faster. She put in long hours, worried all the time, and felt constant fear that she wasn't doing enough. Her parents had never been able to help her ease up on herself, and they had become genuinely afraid she wouldn't be able to maintain the pace she had set nor to endure the demands she put on herself. They feared it was only a matter of time until she burned out completely.

Mirriam-Webster defines perfectionism as "a disposition to regard anything short of perfection as unacceptable; *especially*: the setting of unrealistically demanding goals accompanied by a disposition to regard failure to achieve them as unacceptable and a sign of personal worthlessness." (Merriam Webster.com) Perfectionism is common among the gifted, and while the general population contains about 30% perfectionists, some experts believe that nearly 80% of gifted individuals exhibit perfectionist tendencies. (Natcharian, 2010)

In many ways, it's important to understand what perfectionism is *not* in order to better understand what it is, because perfectionism is not only setting high standards for oneself, nor is it simply a determination to succeed. Unhealthy perfectionism is the feeling that unless one succeeds at all times in all endeavors, one is a failure. Note that people who suffer from perfectionism often cannot separate in their minds the concepts of *doing* and *being* in this area, so not performing some activity perfectly doesn't mean they, "*did* a failure," so to speak, but that they *are* a failure. In their minds, their performance defines their identities.

Moreover, a great many perfectionists feel they must be perfect in every area of life, and that lack of perfection in even one area makes them a failure across the board. They are unable to safely parse activities into those which it is essential to do perfectly and those which allow for some leeway in performance; some perfectionists are unable to consider that there may even *be* activities which have some leeway in expectations. Remember, the intensity exhibited by many gifted people means they're unable to do things by halves, and needing to be perfect is no exception.

People who suffer from perfectionism may have a strong propensity to be triggered by failure events. For these people, any experience of falling short of perfection will immediately call to mind many previous times when the perfectionist felt that he or she failed. This increases the tendency to see the world in all or nothing terms, because when one is in the throes of such an episode, it's true that all one can recall are moments of failure. Triggering reinforces the perception that universal failure is the only alternative to perfection, and this feeling increases the intensity of, and thus the suffering associated with, the experience.

Perfectionism can become debilitating, making it almost impossible for some people who suffer from it to undertake new or challenging activities if there is any chance of not being perfect. They can become paralyzed by the fear of being seen as a complete failure to the point where they won't try anything. Others may refuse to do things in public until they feel they *can* perform perfectly. For example, gifted forums are full of stories of children who refused to even try to read aloud until suddenly, one day, the child could read fluently; they had been so distraught at the thought of failing to read perfectly that they had practiced in secret until they mastered the task. Perfectionists often avoid participating in activities in which perfection is not assured.

Despite the appearances of success that accompany perfectionism, it is a pattern that causes a great deal of suffering. The need to be perfect in all things at all times can be a heavy load to bear, and the impossibility of meeting this goal can lead to discouragement and depression when it is inevitably not achieved. Perfectionism can also be isolating, because the need to be right, to win, or to be the best at all times can drive other people away from individuals who exhibit this trait. Worse, the need to be constantly perfect is frequently a mask for a deep sense of personal worthlessness. Often, perfectionists truly believe they are nothing without their accomplishments. They find it impossible to imagine that who they are, without awards and accolades, is good enough, and this belief can lead to torment throughout their lives. Perfectionism can be painful to live with for both the people suffering from it and those who care about them.

## What It Looks Like

Due to their overwhelming need to succeed, perfectionists often look like very successful people. They do well in school and may excel in their extracurricular activities. Where their perfectionism can be easily seen is in those instances when they fall short of some ideal. They may get less than 100% on a test, or come in second in the science fair, or not make the varsity team, or not get into their first choice college. When faced with situations like these, although they may have performed very well, perfectionists frequently fall apart, describing themselves as utter failures and questioning their very worth as human beings.

Parents may notice that perfectionists are frequently extremely competitive and may view contests in zero-sum terms: there is the winner and there is everyone else, and only the winner gains merit from the competition. They commonly get very down on themselves when they don't win, and they may have a hard time congratulating the person who does. Sometimes when perfectionists win, they may gloat about their victory. Perfectionists often view competition not in terms of doing their best, but as a means to shoring up their sense of worth, and therefore may take it extremely seriously.

You may also notice your perfectionist child avoids trying new things. New activities, especially those which require practice to master, mean that failure is a real possibility, and many perfectionists can't handle being put into that situation. Note that forcing a perfectionist child to try something new without first addressing their perfectionism can be a recipe for disaster, leading to low, or lower, self-esteem, depression, or even suicide in extreme cases. The feelings of worthlessness that accompany failure are real to the perfectionist, no matter how irrational they seem to outsiders, so it's often best to address the perfectionism prior to engaging them in activities they are reluctant to try.

## Strategies to Consider

Tapping is not the only way to approach painful perfectionism. Like many issues, perfectionism responds to a variety of approaches and is often best addressed by a combination of tactics.

For many children, it can be helpful to discuss and model the idea of failure being, at times, acceptable. Children need to see the adults in their lives dealing successfully with failures large and small on a regular basis. As much as parents hate to hear this, it's true that our children do what we do and not what we tell them, so if you are raising a perfectionist, you may wish to carefully consider how you respond to disappointments in your own life.

It may also help to emphasize the notion that perfection isn't attainable across the board. In our house, where admittedly I am the most intense perfectionist, we often discuss the fact that in real life, there are three grades: Pass, Fail, and Exceeds Expectations, more commonly known as You Did Fine, You Didn't Make the Cut, and You Knocked It Out of the Park. We discuss the fact that we have constraints on our time and other resources, which means that we can't possibly Exceed Expectations at everything. However, we get to choose, in each area of our lives, which grade we think is appropriate and devote our time and attention accordingly, so that we're more likely to Exceed Expectations in the areas which are most important to us. However, this means we may merely Pass in some areas, or may even Fail in others. By emphasizing which values and roles are most important to us, we are able to put success and failure into a wider context.

Granted, putting failure in context only gets us so far; the drive to succeed and the feelings that accompany failure are generally too powerful to simply explain away. For people who find this to be true, there are therapeutic approaches that may be beneficial. For example, perfectionism often responds fairly well to cognitive behavioral therapy, which trains people to catch themselves in the act of exhibiting distorted, all-or-nothing thinking, and to reduce the frequency of those episodes over time. Hypnotherapy or guided visualizations may allow children to build neural pathways to deal with lack of perfection with more aplomb. Perfectionism often responds to a variety of approaches.

## EFT to Help

EFT can be a powerful tool in the arsenal to address perfectionism. Using therapeutic tools may allow your child to recognize that he or she is seeing things in a distorted way and may reduce the frequency of these episodes over time, but this doesn't necessarily address the *feelings* associated with the need to succeed or the pain of not reaching your goal, and here EFT can offer significant relief. In addition to offering immediate release of pain, EFT also works directly with deep emotions such as fear of failure and sense of worth, which means that, whether used in conjunction with other tools or used alone, tapping can often reduce perfectionist tendencies extremely well over time.

Remember that if you or your child is experiencing psychological triggering of previous traumatic experiences with failure, addressing triggering may help the situation. You may find relief both by releasing the negative emotions that have surfaced in the immediate term, and by going back and clearing the pain of earlier failure events. In particular, you may wish to use the procedure for clearing old memories to work through as many incidents as the perfectionist can recall when he or she fell short of perfection. Many perfectionists keep a mental list of their shortcomings, so asking them to "Think about a time when you felt you *{failed/ let someone down/ etc}*," will often bring to mind very specific memories that you can clear using the technique discussed in Chapter Three. You may want to keep paper and pencil handy to make notes about related memories that surface during tapping, so you can go back and clear those in subsequent sessions.

I'm including three scripts that may ease the suffering associated with perfectionism. The first is to alleviate the immediate pain of feeling that you have failed, similar to the script for reducing the short term emotions that flare up when you're triggered. The second addresses the fear of failure that so often drives perfectionist behavior. I'm also including a script that speaks to the belief in one's own worthlessness that often underlies perfectionism as a whole.

Note that the first script contains some pretty strong expressions of failure, perhaps more than you're comfortable with your children feeling. The script is written this way because it's easier to release emotions once they've been well and truly acknowledged; however, we will often "water down" our descriptions of how we feel to be more socially acceptable. This may be especially true for perfectionists who see themselves as complete failures when something goes wrong, but who may have been told, implicitly or explicitly, that they "shouldn't" feel this way. By stating things more forcefully than your child may admit to feeling, we're more likely to capture even an extreme current state, making it easier to guide them gently to releasing these feelings by the end of the script.

You can also create a variation on this script if your child actually does get a poor grade on an assignment or in some other way genuinely does fail. For high-achieving children who are unaccustomed to doing poorly, the trauma of receiving a low grade can be immense. This script will enable them to release that pain.

As with all scripts, these are merely starting points. You should use whatever words feel appropriate and can continue to tap at any point along the script if it helps you to clear the incident.

| Point | Statement |
|---|---|
| Karate chop | Even though I feel like I failed, I'm trying to remember to love and accept myself.<br><br>Even though I completely blew it, I'm trying to love and forgive myself.<br><br>Even though I failed and I feel terrible right now, I'm trying to be kind to myself. |
| Above the eye | I failed. |
| Side of the eye | I blew it. |
| Under the eye | My life is one long string of failures. |
| Under the nose | No matter what I do or how hard I try, I'm just a failure. |
| Under the mouth | I hate this feeling! |
| Collarbone | But I let myself down again. |
| Under the arm | I never do anything right. |
| Top of the head | Sometimes people try to tell me I did fine, but I know better. |
| Above the eye | I screwed up. |
| Side of the eye | I wanted to be perfect, but I wasn't. |
| Under the eye | I {came in second/ got a B on my test, etc}. |
| Under the nose | And I am disappointed in myself. |
| Under the mouth | I don't think I did well enough. |
| Collarbone | I wanted {to get an A/ to win, etc}. |
| Under the arm | And I'm really disappointed that it didn't happen. |

| Point | Statement |
|---|---|
| *Top of the head* | And even though it's okay for me to be disappointed, |
| *Above the eye* | It's not okay for me to say terrible things about myself. |
| *Side of the eye* | I don't ALWAYS fail. |
| *Under the eye* | I did well on *{this event}*. |
| *Under the nose* | And I did well *{here}*. |
| *Under the mouth* | For me to say that I always fail means that I'm ignoring a lot of proof that shows otherwise. |
| *Collarbone* | I frequently do well *{in school/ in sports, etc}*. |
| *Under the arm* | I'm not a total failure. |
| *Top of the head* | And even if I don't do as well as I would have liked, |
| *Above the eye* | That doesn't make me a bad person. |
| *Side of the eye* | There's a lot more to me than my accomplishments. |
| *Under the eye* | There's a lot more to me than my *{grades/ awards, etc}*. |
| *Under the nose* | The things that make me a good person have nothing to do with grades, or coming in first. |
| *Under the mouth* | I'm good enough without those things. |
| *Collarbone* | So I'm choosing to release my hurt feelings. |
| *Under the arm* | I'm choosing to release my disappointment. |
| *Top of the head* | I'm letting all the bad feelings go. |
| *Above the eye* | I'm taking a deep breath |

| Point | Statement |
|---|---|
| Side of the eye | And allowing myself to know that not reaching my goal doesn't make me a bad person. |
| Under the eye | I forgive myself for not achieving my goal. |
| Under the nose | I forgive myself for not being perfect. |
| Under the mouth | I allow myself to know I don't have to be perfect. |
| Collarbone | Releasing any remaining anger, disappointment, or hurt |
| Under the arm | From every cell in my body. |
| Top of the head | I allow myself to know that I'm okay. |
| *Take a deep breath in through your nose...* *Hold it for a few seconds...* *Release it slowly through your mouth.* | |

The next script deals with fear of failure, which is common among perfectionists. It can also be used before beginning or undertaking a frightening or intimidating event, such as before a test or prior to tryouts for the school play.

I created this script based on the ideas presented in the excellent book by Dr. Susan Jeffers, *Feel the Fear and Do It Anyway*, which I highly recommend, particularly if you or your children are prone to anxiety. Her contention is that we do not fear what we *believe* we fear, but that we actually are afraid we're unable to *handle* the things we fear. For example, many gifted children express fear of growing up, but she would argue that they actually fear that they cannot *handle* growing up. In fact, according to Dr. Jeffers, all fears can be reduced to the single fear of our inability to handle what may come.

EFT can be extremely valuable when addressing fears of all types, from fear of something happening to a loved one to anxiety about performing in public. We can use tapping to acknowledge our surface fear, we can allow ourselves to admit our deeper fears of being unable to handle the situation if or when it arises, we can release our fear, and then we can replace it with confidence in our ability to deal with whatever life brings. Using this formula, the script below can be adjusted to address nearly any kind of fear.

| Point | Statement |
|---|---|
| Karate chop | Even though I'm afraid because I may not succeed at {what I'm about to do}, I love and accept myself just as I am.<br><br>Even though I'm scared, because what if I fail? And what if people know? I choose to treat myself with kindness and compassion.<br><br>Even though I'm really afraid to fail, I forgive myself for feeling afraid and decide to love myself anyhow. |
| Above the eye | I'm scared. |
| Side of the eye | I may fail at {this thing I'm about to do} and that would be awful. |
| Under the eye | I hate failing! |

| Point | Statement |
|---|---|
| Under the nose | What if I fail, and someone finds out? |
| Under the mouth | What if someone laughs at me? |
| Collarbone | What if people think I'm a loser? |
| Under the arm | What if *I* think I'm a loser? |
| Top of the head | I don't want to fail. |
| Above the eye | I don't think I want to even DO *(this thing)*! |
| Side of the eye | I'm really afraid of failing. |
| Under the eye | I guess most people are afraid of failing. |
| Under the nose | It's always a little bit scary to do something new, or hard. |
| Under the mouth | But maybe it's easier for other people than it is for me. |
| Collarbone | Or maybe not. |
| Under the arm | Maybe everyone has to do things that are frightening. |
| Top of the head | Maybe everyone has to do things they might fail at. |
| Above the eye | Yes, but I can't handle failure! |
| Side of the eye | So maybe that means that what I'm afraid of isn't failing... |
| Under the eye | Maybe I'm afraid I can't handle failure. |
| Under the nose | I can't handle what people will say. |
| Under the mouth | I can't handle what people will think. |
| Collarbone | (Although if I'm honest, I don't really KNOW what people think!) |

## Perfectionism

| Point | Statement |
|---|---|
| *Under the arm* | I'm afraid I can't handle it. |
| *Top of the head* | Except that I'm pretty sure I CAN handle it. |
| *Above the eye* | I can handle whatever comes. |
| *Side of the eye* | I'm capable, resilient, and resourceful. |
| *Under the eye* | I have people who will help and support me, no matter what happens. |
| *Under the nose* | I can handle it. |
| *Under the mouth* | I WILL handle it. |
| *Collarbone* | I'll handle whatever comes. |
| *Under the arm* | I'll be okay, no matter what happens. |
| *Top of the head* | No matter the outcome, I'm going to be okay. |
| *Take a deep breath in through your nose...* <br> *Hold it for a few seconds...* <br> *Release it slowly through your mouth.* | |

The third tapping script gets at one of the deeper issues that often drives perfectionist behavior, namely the belief that one isn't good enough without external success and validation. Note that this is a belief, which makes it different from many of the issues we've addressed so far. Previously, we've been working with particular memories or specific emotions, but beliefs are much more general thought patterns. Beliefs are thoughts we have over and over again, and usually our beliefs are grounded in some sort of evidence. Something happens which seems to support some conclusion we draw about that event, and with enough proof to back us up, we create a belief.

Obviously, the beliefs we develop vary widely, depending on our life experiences. Some beliefs are valuable, helping us to be the people we want to be. If we have positive encounters with volunteerism, for example, we might come to believe that we make the world a better place by donating our time to certain causes. Others may be developed through the accumulation of painful evidence, but the beliefs themselves may still be valuable, such as a belief that lying to our loved ones causes them pain and should therefore be avoided. Yet other beliefs we hold are objectively false, but because of the evidence we've accumulated over time, we believe them anyway, such as the idea that we can't trust anyone outside our families. With enough evidence, we can build beliefs about anything.

Although most people view their beliefs as unchanging, they actually fluctuate through time. As we grow and as our circumstances change, it's very common to find that beliefs which kept us safe and happy in one place or with one group of people don't apply in new situations. For instance, we may learn as children that it's unsafe for us to talk about our unusual interests at school, but changing schools may mean that even though we still hold the belief, it isn't actually true any longer. As new information and evidence become available to us, most of us instinctively reconsider the beliefs which shape our behavior. We may decide that while it's still pointless to talk about our passions with most people we know, it's safe to share our interests with select individuals, for example. We commonly revise our beliefs to fit our new circumstances.

However, some beliefs are more fixed than others. Because we knew these things to be "true" at one time, we tend to accept that they'll be true throughout our lives. They can be difficult to modify based solely on new evidence, and this is especially common for beliefs about our identities. Once we have it in our heads that, "I'm a person who..." it can be extremely difficult to shake this conviction, even if it is objectively false. Most of us are naturally resistant to changing how we think of ourselves, and while it can be done, it often takes conscious effort to identify our beliefs and to determine which ones continue to help us be our best selves.

Even if we're able to identify beliefs that no longer serve us, we still have the sometimes monumental task of changing them. Revising what we honestly believe about ourselves and the world can be an uphill battle, because so often, simply knowing something in our heads doesn't make it feel true in our hearts. EFT can play a crucial role in helping us to alter our beliefs, because tapping can enable us to understand material in new ways. In particular, when we're able to use tapping to remove the pain associated with our memories, the lessons we draw from those experiences will change. We begin to see that our experiences may not "prove" what we thought they proved.

Therefore, as a rule, when we decide to dismantle a belief that isn't serving us, it's often more productive to tap on the "proof" that the belief is true, rather than the belief itself. The creator of EFT, Gary Craig, likens a belief to a table. The table top is the belief, and the memories and experiences which support that belief are the legs of the table. Tapping on the table top may or may not bring it down, but taking out the legs, one at a time, will surely collapse the table sooner or later.

What does all this mean for your child's belief that he or she isn't good enough without external success and validation? It means a few things. First, if your child is one who holds this belief, it's worth beginning by tapping on the issue directly. It may be enough to clear the belief, or at least begin the process of dislodging it. The script I've included below attacks the table top, if you will – the belief itself – and also targets some of the sources of resistance that crop up when we consider updating our beliefs. It's a good place to start.

Second, you shouldn't be surprised if this tapping doesn't cause the belief to clear. It's common that using EFT on broad issues doesn't get results. If this happens, work with your child to figure out what pieces of evidence he or she holds that support this belief by asking, "Can you think of a time you felt you weren't good enough, just as you are?" Make a list of the answers and then tap on the specific memories that come up, one at a time, using the technique discussed in Chapter Three for clearing traumatic memories. This should clear the belief by addressing the supporting pieces of evidence, or, using Gary Craig's analogy, by removing the legs that hold up the table.

*Perfectionism*

Third, if this process sounds overwhelming, you may wish to contact an EFT practitioner. Helping clients clear their limiting beliefs is bread-and-butter work for the people in this field, and they'll be happy to help your child clear this old belief so he or she is better able to see his or her worth as a human being, unrelated to extrinsic measures of success or failure.

As with all the scripts provided, this is intended to be simply a starting point for your family. Use your own words, add thoughts as they arise, and spend more time on certain phrases if they resonate for your children. Also, you may wish to make note of this script for use with other beliefs you or your kids decide to revise. You can modify it to address any belief, ranging from "Nobody likes me," to "People are stupid." Having the ability to fundamentally alter how we and our children see ourselves and the world can be a powerful gift, because knowing how to adjust inaccurate self-perceptions and negative worldviews can reduce or eliminate a great deal of suffering over time.

| *Point* | Statement |
|---|---|
| *Karate chop* | Even though I feel like I'm not good enough, I want to love and accept myself.<br><br>Although I feel like the real me just isn't enough without having something to back me up or make me look better, I accept how I feel in this moment. |

| Point | Statement |
|---|---|
| | Even though it feels like I'm not good enough as I am, I'm trying very hard to love and accept myself anyway. |
| Above the eye | I believe I'm not good enough. |
| Side of the eye | I'm just not enough. |
| Under the eye | I feel like people look at me and wonder, "Is that it?" |
| Under the nose | I want so badly to be loved and respected for who I am, |
| Under the mouth | But I feel like I need to constantly prove that I'm worthy of being loved. |
| Collarbone | I feel that unless I do something special, or something to please other people, they'll think I'm not worth having around. |
| Under the arm | I don't think who I am is good enough for other people. |
| Top of the head | I don't think who I am is good enough for myself. |
| Above the eye | And even though I'm allowed to feel this way, |
| Side of the eye | I need to remember that these feelings are LIES! |
| Under the eye | This may be what I believe, |
| Under the nose | But just because I believe it, doesn't make it true! |
| Under the mouth | A belief is just a thought I tell myself over and over. |
| Collarbone | And I can learn to change how I think about myself. |

*Perfectionism*

| Point | Statement |
|---|---|
| *Under the arm* | I can learn to see myself differently. |
| *Top of the head* | I'm willing to see myself differently. |
| *Above the eye* | And I am worthy of seeing myself differently than I did in the past. |
| *Under the eye* | The truth is, I AM good enough. |
| *Under the nose* | I don't need to do anything special to be good enough. |
| *Under the mouth* | I don't have to prove anything. |
| *Collarbone* | I know I'm good enough because I'm here. |
| *Under the arm* | It's part of being human. |
| *Top of the head* | All people are worthy and deserving of love and respect, and that includes me. |
| *Above the eye* | It's not true that there are seven billion people on this planet who are good enough… |
| *Side of the eye* | Except for THAT ONE right there! |
| *Under the eye* | I'm enough just as I am. |
| *Under the nose* | I don't have to earn other people's love. |
| *Under the mouth* | I am loved for who I am. |
| *Collarbone* | And I'm learning to love myself for who I am. |
| *Under the arm* | I'm learning to accept myself just the way I am. |
| *Top of the head* | The real me is good enough. |
| *Above the eye* | So I'm letting go of all my doubts about whether I'm good enough. |
| *Side of the eye* | I'm letting go of all my fears that I may not be good enough. |

*Tapping for the Gifted Child*

| Point | Statement |
|---|---|
| *Under the eye* | I'm releasing my fear from every cell in my body, |
| *Under the nose* | And all the way back through my past. |
| *Under the mouth* | I'm choosing to remember I have nothing to prove. |
| *Collarbone* | I'm allowing myself to know that who I am is completely good enough. |
| *Under the arm* | I am loved. |
| *Top of the head* | And who I am is enough. |
| *Take a deep breath in through your nose...* *Hold it for a few seconds...* *Release it slowly through your mouth.* ||

CHAPTER EIGHT

# Isolation

Melissa's mother hid a sigh as her daughter came home in tears, again. Her mom could still hear the shouts and laughter of the other children, but apparently the neighborhood soccer game had not gone well for Melissa.

"They changed the rules!" Melissa yelled. "We agreed on the rules and there were two time outs per team but then Andre took a third time out. When I said he couldn't do that, he said he could! And everyone agreed with him! You can't change the rules after the game starts. That's not fair!"

Melissa's mother wasn't sure what to say. On the one hand, her daughter was right that changing the rules mid-game wasn't exactly fair, but being a stickler for rules meant that Melissa didn't have any friends in the neighborhood, even though all the local kids were in the same pull-out program in school. She was always telling on the other children, or getting upset when people did things she thought were unfair. Her mother wished Melissa could relax a little bit, maybe let things slide once in a while. How was she ever going to have friends if all she cared about were the rules?

At some point in their lives, virtually all gifted individuals find themselves feeling misunderstood by the general population simply because they are different from neurotypical individuals. In some cases, it is their intensity or their vocabularies that make them stand out; in others, their passion for unusual topics or their sense of humor sets them apart. For most gifted people, the very fact that they are gifted makes them feel alone.

> Not every gifted child is socially awkward, a poor athlete, or any of the other concepts we might associate with them. Nearly all, however, feel some degree of loneliness and isolation—even the popular, athletic ones. There is some part of themselves that they cannot share with their peers: the part that wants to talk about the finer points of particle physics, for instance, or that just blew through the collected works of Jane Austen in a week. They've learned to silence it, because no one understands, or because it will make teachers and parents expect even more of them than they already give. (Cornwell, 2015)

There is a common misperception that if we don't *tell* kids they're gifted, somehow they won't know that they're different from other children, but they frequently, instinctively know it and may feel that way from a very young age. They may notice that they like things the other kids don't enjoy, or may not enjoy activities other children their age do, or may be mystified by the behavior of their classmates. Even when participating in similar activities,

## Isolation

their behavior is often markedly different. For example, when my daughter was four, we went to a local park with several families who had children around the same age. All the children spent the day playing with sticks: everyone else raced around the playground, pretend sword-fighting, while my daughter built anatomically correct skeletons of dinosaurs, proudly pointing out the pine cones she had found to represent the hip joint of the theropod. There was no doubt in anyone's mind that one of those kids was not like the others; in fact, it's frequently through watching interactions like these that parents first begin to learn how different their children are.

The more gifted the child, the more likely it is that he or she will experience isolation. Children who are mildly or moderately gifted will often be able to find at least some common interests with classmates and can often – though by no means always – find someone they relate to in school or the community. Extremely gifted children, however, may find it almost impossible to relate to children of the same age, who may be learning at a level several years behind them and whose interests may differ accordingly. Many gifted children find intellectual peers among older children or adults, but for some profoundly gifted children, even adults may not understand their thinking. Extreme abilities frequently come with equally extreme loneliness when it seems that no one understands you.

For most of us, the ideal solution to isolation is to find an actual friend, but this can be a real challenge for gifted children. The initial criterion gifted children generally use when seeking someone with whom to become friends is someone whose current abilities are similar to their own, for, as Miraca Gross said, "Children tend to choose friends on the basis of similarities in mental age, rather than chronological age." (Gross, 2002) However, as we discussed in Chapter One, one of the most prominent traits of gifted children is their asynchrony, or their tendency to develop in different areas of their lives at different rates. Asynchronous development is often a complicating factor when gifted children look for people to whom they can relate, because two gifted children who have the same mental age may vary significantly in other areas. In order to find a friend, gifted children generally need to find someone with whom they are compatible on many levels at once, and for some, this can be extremely hard to accomplish.

Another reason gifted children may struggle to find friends is because their ideas of friendship may differ significantly from those of other children their age. Researcher Miraca Gross has done a lot of work identifying the various types of friendship exhibited by children, ranging from the "play partner," the child who is my friend because we play together, all the way up to the "sure shelter," a deep and lasting relationship of trust and sharing. Children's views of friendship move sequentially through the various stages, and gifted children very often move to more complex views of friendship than neurotypical children of the same age. (Gross, 2002) Gifted children, therefore, may be looking for interactions with their peers that their peers cannot even conceive of, making a mismatch almost guaranteed.

In many cases, the feeling of being alone in the world can be overwhelming. Feeling that no one understands you can be devastating for anyone, regardless of age or level of giftedness, or lack thereof; we all want to feel understood. However, due to the many ways they are different from the general population, gifted individuals may accumulate considerable evidence from an early age that they're unlikely to find people with whom they connect. They may build early beliefs around the idea that they are alone or different and may feel hopeless about the possibility of the situation ever changing, and due to the overall intensity that is so common among the gifted, the loneliness and hopelessness they experience may also be extreme.

Unsurprisingly, feelings of isolation can become exacerbated in gifted teenagers. People of all ages need peers and friends, but the primary developmental task of teenagers is to separate from their families of origin and build a strong community of peers in preparation for moving out and living on their own. However, many gifted teens find it difficult or impossible to create these communities when they live and go to school among people who don't understand them. They may desperately want to connect with others, but they may find themselves feeling more and more like outsiders when others their age form groups without them due to their differences.

It's important not to blame the victim when dealing with feelings of isolation. Sometimes, people in the community, possibly even including teachers or coaches, may suggest that the reason your children are lonely is because they are "weird," or some other derogatory term, but it's important that you advocate for your children's right to be themselves. Gifted children *are* different from other children, by definition; that doesn't mean there's anything wrong with them being who or how they are, nor does it mean that they should be expected to be something they're not in order to fit in. Children need to be valued for who they are in order to grow up healthy and well-adjusted.

Also note that feelings of isolation should not be ignored. Feeling alone in the world, especially if it's accompanied by a belief that the situation cannot or will not change, can be a powerful driver of depression in gifted youth, and unfortunately can contribute to suicidal thoughts or actions. It can be difficult to help your children find people who understand and appreciate them, but it's well worth the effort, for their sakes.

## What It Looks Like

It's not uncommon for gifted children to tell their parents when they feel isolated, but expressions of their children's isolation and loneliness can be among the most heartbreaking words many parents ever hear. Hearing lines like, "Mommy, nobody likes me," or, "Why don't I have friends?" can be devastating for a parent. If you are one of the parents who hears them, please remember that you haven't done anything wrong; you're fortunate that your child feels safe enough to come to you with his or her problems, and together you can work to address the situation.

Not all children are able or willing to be so direct about how they feel, so it may fall to you to notice feelings of isolation. You may notice your child routinely plays alone when there are other children nearby, or perhaps you observe that your child begins playtime by interacting with other children, but as time goes on, the other children tire of your child's elaborate game and run off. You may notice that your child is often alone.

However, gifted children are complex, and being alone may or may not be an indicator of feeling isolated. Especially if they are introverted, many gifted children genuinely enjoy solitude and really do prefer solo imaginative play, building with Legos©, or reading, to spending time with other children. Others engage in these pursuits only because they are preferable to spending time with people who don't understand. You may have to be persistent in figuring out which is the case for your child.

Another indicator that your children may feel isolated is if they spend most of their time with people of very different ages. Many gifted children who don't connect with their age peers will choose to interact with adults or much younger children. Talking to adults allows gifted children to experience peer-level conversation, even if the adult sometimes has to "talk down" to the child's level, whereas younger children allow the gifted child to feel important, helpful, or admired, albeit without much component of being truly understood. If you find that your child always chooses to be with much older or much younger people, you may wish to check whether he or she feels isolated.

You should be aware that children may try to disguise feelings of isolation. They may feel shame at being different, which may make it difficult for them to admit that they don't fit in. They may also experience hopelessness, feeling that there is nothing that can be done about the situation, so there's no point in discussing it. Also, as we discussed in Chapter One, gifted children are often extremely sensitive to their environment, and their sensitivity to your feelings may mean they hide their emotions so as to not alarm or distress you. Buried or disguised feelings of isolation are very real, however, so you may wish to introduce the topic yourself if your child does not.

## Strategies to Consider

When gifted children feel isolated, the real solution is to help them find "their people." All children need peers who understand them to help them grow up knowing there's nothing wrong with them, and for most gifted children, these peers are other gifted children. Other gifted children are the ones who are more likely to have read the same books your kids have, or share your child's love of robotics, or have a similar sense of humor, and for children, making these connections for the first time can be validating and empowering. As a parent, you may find it challenging to help your child find those gifted peers, but it's crucial that you make that effort, because having even a single friend can significantly affect your child's quality of life. There are a number of ways to find other families with gifted children, and some of these are listed in the Resources section.

Remember that your children may need to find a variety of people to serve as peers in a variety of settings. Some children have a harder time than others finding people who share their deep and sometimes eclectic interests, so it may be necessary to find different people who can talk to your kids about their various passions. Joining community organizations or clubs may give your children the chance to meet people who share specific interests, and it can be exciting for kids to talk about their passions with people who are equally excited about them, even if these individuals may not become close friends in other areas of life. While it might be simpler to have your child connect with a single person for all their interests, this isn't always possible; however, it's still valuable for them to have people with whom they can share even one or two interests. Being understood is a deeply soothing balm for people who often feel out of sync with the world.

Another tactic you may wish to use when dealing with your child's feelings of isolation may be to simply discuss with your children the fact that things do, often, get better with time. First, everyone will grow up, so the same-age peers whose social or emotional development currently lags behind your child's will catch up, making it easier to form connections. Miraca Gross said, "Leta Hollingworth (1936) believed that the social isolation experienced by many highly gifted children was most acute between the ages of 4 and 9. My own findings strongly support this. Children of IQ 160+ tend to begin the search for "the sure shelter" - friendships of complete trust, honesty and fidelity - four or five years before their age-peers even enter this stage. Indeed, in my study exceptionally and profoundly gifted girls aged 6 and 7 already displayed conceptions of friendship which do not develop in children of average ability until age 11 or 12." (Gross, Tips for Parents: Gifted Children's Friendships, 2006) It's important for children, and their parents, to remember that the gap between what your gifted child is looking for in a friend, and what more neurotypical children nearby are looking for in a friend, will become closer over time.

It can also be important to remind children that once people are grown, they aren't grouped by chronological age but by interests and abilities. So much of our culture segregates children solely by age, and this can make it seem to children that the whole world is broken down that way. However, once your children are done with school, it will likely be easier for them to find and spend time with people with common interests and whose company they enjoy. Hopefully they will take some comfort from knowing this is not an unending situation.

## EFT to Help

While helping your children to find "their people" is a fairly permanent solution to the problem of them not having people who understand, this solution may also be years away. To help address the pain of the situation in the short term, I've included a few tapping routines below.

*Isolation*

Also remember that if your child has had a specific, negative experience with feeling isolated, you can guide him or her to tap on that particular memory using the technique for clearing a memory included in Chapter Three.

The first routine in this chapter is designed to help you acknowledge and release the general negative feelings associated with isolation. As always, these scripts are here simply to get you started. Use whatever words land for your child and continue to tap at any point along the script if it helps to clear the emotions.

| Point | Statement |
|---|---|
| *Karate chop* | Even though no one understands me, I love and accept myself anyway. |
| | Even though I feel all alone sometimes, I completely accept who I am. |
| | Even though I feel *{hurt/ sad/ angry/ etc}* because I don't fit in *{at school/ in Sunday school/ with the neighborhood kids/ etc}*, I deeply and completely love and accept myself. |
| *Above the eye* | I don't fit in. |
| *Side of the eye* | No one understands me. |
| *Under the eye* | I like things the other kids don't like. |
| *Under the nose* | I don't like to do what they do. |
| *Under the mouth* | I'm just different. |

| Point | Statement |
|---|---|
| Collarbone | And I hate being different! |
| Under the arm | I hate feeling like I'll never belong. |
| Top of the head | I'm sad that I don't fit in. |
| Above the eye | It hurts to know that everyone thinks I'm {weird/ different/ etc} just because I don't work like they do! |
| Side of the eye | And I'm afraid I may never find the kind of friends I want. |
| Under the eye | I just want a friend who understands me. |
| Under the nose | Everyone does, I guess. |
| Under the mouth | I know I'm not the only one. |
| Collarbone | But it doesn't always help to know there are others in the same boat. |
| Under the arm | It doesn't make me any less lonely. |
| Top of the head | But even though I feel lonely, |
| Above the eye | I need to remember that lonely is all I am. |
| Side of the eye | I am not {weird, etc} even if I'm not like everyone else. |
| Under the eye | I don't have to be like everyone else. |
| Under the nose | It's okay to be different. |
| Under the mouth | It's okay to have my own interests and my own ways of doing things. |
| Collarbone | I don't have to be like everyone else. |
| Under the arm | The world values people who innovate – inventors, entrepreneurs... |

*Isolation*

| Point | Statement |
|---|---|
| *Top of the head* | And the world will value ME! |
| *Above the eye* | Maybe not the people I see every day {*at school/ in Sunday school/ in our neighborhood/ etc*}. |
| *Side of the eye* | But there will be lots of people in my life who see how amazing and marvelous I am. |
| *Under the eye* | People who admire my mind and {*sense of humor/ creativity/ other trait that people don't currently appreciate*}. |
| *Under the nose* | I WILL find people who understand me. |
| *Under the mouth* | And in the meantime, I will remember that other people don't determine my worth. |
| *Collarbone* | I'm a worthwhile person even if other people can't always see it. |
| *Under the arm* | So I'm letting go of my hurt feelings. |
| *Top of the head* | I'm letting go of my sadness. |
| *Above the eye* | I'm letting go of my fear. |
| *Side of the eye* | I'm releasing all my feelings of being misunderstood and alone. |
| *Under the eye* | I'm choosing to remember that there are some people who think I'm great right now, |
| *Under the nose* | And I will find others in time. |
| *Under the mouth* | I will have friends. |
| *Collarbone* | There will be lots of people who are thankful for the chance to call themselves my friend. |
| *Under the arm* | I'm letting go of any remaining sadness and fear. |

| Point | Statement |
|---|---|
| Top of the head | And I'm allowing myself to feel at peace. |
| Take a deep breath in through your nose... <br> Hold it for a few seconds... <br> Release it slowly through your mouth. | |

Frequently, issues of isolation, like issues related to perfectionism, are based in our beliefs. Children build beliefs about themselves and their world based on their interactions with other kids, and if your children are in an area with a poor social fit, there may be a great deal of evidence to support their beliefs around isolation. Statements like, "Nobody likes me," or, "No one understands me," often become the deeply held beliefs of isolated gifted children. Far too many parents of gifted children have heard these heartrending words without feeling like they have an effective way to comfort their children, so the rest of this chapter will continue the work we began in Chapter Seven on beliefs as we address this aspect of isolation.

The first step in addressing statements like this is to recognize – and help your child to recognize – that they are beliefs rather than facts. Just as scientists use data as evidence to draw conclusions they believe to be true, so, too, are the beliefs we hold about our lives the *conclusions* we draw from the events that happen to us. The events themselves provide the data which support our beliefs. One way to help your child see that these are beliefs, therefore, might be to ask for their evidence. For example,

*Isolation*

if your child comes to you and says, "Nobody likes me," you might ask whether this statement is absolutely true, and how they know. In order to prove their point, they will have to marshal evidence to back up their assertion, and at that point, you can remind them that any conclusion drawn from evidence is, by definition, not a fact, but a belief.

Knowing that you are dealing with a belief is important for a few reasons. First, it's crucial to remember that sometimes, even the best minds draw the wrong conclusion from the evidence before them. Sometimes people draw the wrong conclusion because they have incomplete data, and this is frequently a problem in interpersonal interactions. For example, there may be things going on in someone's life of which we are unaware, that may cause them to behave toward us in hurtful ways even if they like us very much.

At other times, people draw the wrong conclusion because they misinterpret the data they have. For instance, teasing behavior is frequently interpreted as having been intentionally hurtful when it was not meant that way. It's important to remember that the conclusions – beliefs – we infer from the incidents in our lives do not automatically reflect the correct interpretation of events, no matter how strongly we may feel we're right.

Another reason it is important to understand when we are working with beliefs is because this affects the language we use when speaking of them. As you already know, EFT works best when used with particular incidents and specific language, so helping your child to refine his or her beliefs can give you much more precise language to use in tapping scripts. For example, you can help your child to move from the statement, "Nobody likes me," to the more accurate statement, "I *believe* that nobody likes me." If you were to ask again whether the statement is absolutely true, hopefully you would be able to point out that if no one else, *you* like your child, so perhaps an even more precise statement would be, "I believe nobody *my age* likes me." In fact, you could ask *again* whether the statement is absolutely true, and maybe the answer will be, "No, So-and-So likes me," so perhaps a more accurate statement would be, "I *often feel* like nobody my age likes me," or even, "I wish I had more friends." By refining the language used to describe the belief, you and your child have created a more precise statement which is more useful for EFT work.

In fact, you may wish to have your child tap on this new statement directly by putting it into the setup statement of a new routine.

| Point | Statement |
|---|---|
| *Karate chop* | Even though I wish I had more friends, I love and accept myself.<br><br>Even though I wish I had more friends who really get me, I accept myself just as I am.<br><br>Even though I wish I had more friends, and I'm sad that I don't, I deeply and completely love and accept myself today. |

*Isolation*

| Point | Statement |
|---|---|
| *Above the eye* | I wish I had more friends. |
| *Side of the eye* | It feels like there *{is no one/ are very few people}* who understand me. |
| *Under the eye* | I'm often lonely, and that makes me sad. |
| *Under the nose* | I'm allowed to feel sad. |
| *Under the mouth* | Being lonely is no fun. |
| *Collarbone* | But I know this won't last forever. |
| *Under the arm* | There are people who will be glad to know me, |
| *Top of the head* | Even if I haven't found as many of them yet as I would like. |
| *Above the eye* | I acknowledge my sadness and let it pass through me. |
| *Side of the eye* | I will not hold on to feelings of sadness or loneliness. |
| *Under the eye* | It's okay to feel this way, but I don't need to dwell on it. |
| *Under the nose* | I know that I will have more friends in the future, when *{other kids get older/ I change schools/ etc}*. |
| *Under the mouth* | For now, I'm proud that I'm being true to who I am, even if I'm lonely for a while, |
| *Collarbone* | Because I'm a great person even if the other kids can't always see it. |
| *Under the arm* | I'm letting all my sadness go, |
| *Top of the head* | And allowing myself to feel peaceful and calm. |

*Tapping for the Gifted Child*

| Point | Statement |
|---|---|
| Take a deep breath in through your nose... | |
| Hold it for a few seconds... | |
| Release it slowly through your mouth. | |

CHAPTER NINE

# Depression

Mahala's father stared at his daughter's report card, speechless.

Mahala loved school. She loved to learn and had always been a straight-A student. She had sometimes found elementary and middle school a little tedious, but she had enthusiastically embraced the transition to high school, joining several clubs, signing up for the most challenging courses she could, and even trying out for not one, but two, sports teams. Her dad had been proud of her ability to fit in and make the most of her education.

During the past few months, however, Mahala hadn't seemed as enthusiastic about school as usual. She no longer talked about her classes, she had decided not to try out for the fall play, and she had actually quit the field hockey team, saying she was too busy to play.

But her father couldn't imagine what she'd been too busy *doing* to play hockey, because she certainly hadn't been studying. Instead of her usual slate of A's and accolades, Mahala's report card showed B's and even C's. It was unheard of!

When he asked her what was happening, her only answer was, "I don't know. I just don't care about school anymore." Her father was at a loss. What was going on with his daughter?

Clinical depression is a serious illness. If you or your children suffer from depression, please do not hesitate to consult mental health professionals who can help to alleviate your, or your children's, suffering. This disease should be taken and treated seriously.

Depression is an illness which includes emotional disturbances among its symptoms, frequently including sadness, anxiety, guilt, and reduced self-worth. (World Health Organization, 2015) Although EFT may not cure the core causes of the disease, it's important to discuss because depression is common in the gifted world and tapping may be used effectively to reduce the impact of painful emotions, thereby reducing the suffering associated with the condition.

Depression is among the most common mental disorders in the world, and an estimated 350 million people suffer from it worldwide. (World Health Organization, 2015) It can be debilitating, making it difficult or impossible for children and adolescents to succeed in school, for them to sustain interest in favored activities, or at times, for them to successfully function in society. At its worst, depression can be fatal, and sadly, nearly 4,600 teens commit suicide in the United States each year. (Statistics Brain, 2015) Depression should not be taken lightly.

In the general population, nearly 12% of teenagers experience depression at any one time (National Institutes of Health, 2014), and nearly 20% of teens experience major depression before they reach adulthood. (I Need a Lighthouse, 2015) The statistics tell us that gifted children and adolescents are no more likely than other teens to experience depression (Neihart, Reis, Robinson, & Moon, 2002). However, in my personal experience, the frequency of depression among gifted youths is much, much higher than one in five, and the more gifted the individual, the more likely he or she is to experience some form of depression prior to adulthood.

There are nearly endless ways gifted children and teens may experience emotional fallout from being gifted, and virtually everything discussed in this book can spark or intensify depression. Feeling unchallenged, feeling like a fraud, feeling like a failure for any number of reasons, feeling alone... all of these emotions can contribute to the experience of depression. Although depression is by no means limited to gifted individuals, there are a great many aspects of the gifted experience which may initiate or exacerbate a depressed state.

Although the circumstances which give rise to it can vary widely, the pain of depression is very real. In fact, in its most basic form, depression may be thought of as an ongoing situation in which pain overwhelms the coping mechanisms to deal with that pain. You may wish to think of it as a balance scale with *Things that Cause Pain* on one side, and *Things that Help Me Deal with Pain* on the other. As long as our pain and ability to handle pain are in balance, we generally function without depression; however, once the pain side of the balance outweighs the coping mechanism side, depression can result. It may be that a single, enormously painful event overpowers our capacity to cope, or that a number of small, negative experiences cumulatively overwhelm our ability to deal with pain. At other times, the pain we're dealing with may not change, but depression may result when coping mechanisms are removed, for example, when a favorite teacher goes on maternity leave, or when a dear friend moves away.

Even the changes in brain chemistry associated with depression can be seen as affecting one or both sides of this balance. A lack of certain neurotransmitters can make negative experiences seem more painful and overwhelming, increasing our pain, or they can reduce our abilities to cope with issues that arise. We may find that we lack the energy to take care of ourselves or to do the things which can reduce the symptoms of depression, such as eating well or taking a walk in the sunshine. Brain chemistry imbalances can contribute to the sense that pain is overtaking our ability to handle it.

Although this imbalance between pain and coping mechanisms may exist for anyone, whether or not they are gifted, there are a number of ways gifted individuals show even more propensity for depression based on this model.

For example, depression may strike even extremely young gifted children, whose coping

## Depression

mechanisms may not yet be well developed. Even very young children may experience the negative ramifications of being gifted, and the more gifted they are, the earlier depression may strike. They may find themselves enduring a poor social or academic fit as early as preschool, or they may find themselves intellectually understanding things they haven't the emotional capacity to handle. In either case, their pain may outstrip their abilities to cope with it, and they may find themselves reeling and unable to recover without specific assistance.

Gifted people of all ages are also commonly overwhelmed by the magnitude of global issues such as climate change, economic collapse, or social injustice. At times, the nuanced scientific or geopolitical situations that gifted individuals can see will provoke terror or despair, creating great amounts of pain. Having the intellectual capacity to understand these problems, with only limited ability to affect the behavior of other people, can easily overwhelm a gifted child's ability to deal with the pain of the situation and result in depression.

Gifted individuals are also prone to what is commonly referred to as "existential depression," which arises when there are no good answers to some of the deepest questions of existence, centering on life, death, choices, and meaning. "What is the meaning of life?" or "What happens when we die?" can be distressing questions for anyone to ponder, and the lack of satisfactory answers can create pain that overwhelms our abilities to cope. Frequently, gifted individuals are naturally deep thinkers, and may therefore find themselves confronting these questions at several points in their lives, potentially including when quite young. The death of a family member or pet may also trigger these questions among gifted children, whose intellectual capacity renders them able to cognitively understand death without the emotional resources to deal with it.

Existential depression is also frequently triggered by decision points in gifted people's lives. For instance, choosing which high schools or colleges to apply to, or which career to pursue, can be fraught times for gifted individuals. It's not uncommon that gifted children are good at many different things, and they may therefore have a difficult time choosing between equally appealing options, such as being a violinist or a neurobiologist. The necessity of rejecting possible paths may cause gifted kids to question their purpose in life, often yielding more pain than they are capable of dealing with. Thus, at times, existential depression may result from some of the basic qualities of giftedness.

Regardless of what triggers depression in gifted children and teens, one last crucial thing to remember is that depression doesn't only create pain in the people who have the disorder. Watching a loved one struggle against depression can cause great suffering in friends and family. If you care about someone with this condition, please take care of yourself, too, and seek support if you need it.

## What It Looks Like

Although most people equate depression with low mood, depression in children and adolescents can look very different from depression in adults. For example, depressed children and teens may display an angry or irritable mood more than despondency or apathy. A depressed child or teenager may be cranky, aggressive, easily annoyed, or prone to angry outbursts. He or she may also be extremely sensitive to criticism, because depression can increase feelings of low self-worth, and any critical comments may be seen as excessively painful when a child is already feeling low and vulnerable.

It is also common for children and teenagers suffering from depression to complain about physical issues such as headaches or stomachaches. These ailments may not indicate a desire to avoid school or other unpleasant experiences but may actually be physical symptoms of the illness.

Note that gifted children and teens may intentionally attempt to hide their depression from family, friends, and even professionals. They may deliberately try to maintain a cheerful demeanor or even lie about their emotional state. As P. Susan Jackson and Jean Peterson say, "Several factors appeared to contribute to this masking phenomenon, including shame for being incapacitated and unable to resolve their dilemma; depression's signature cognitive confusion, which disengaged their coping mechanisms; and fear of harming others with their toxic state." (Jackson & Peterson, 2004) This effort to hide depression can make it even harder to discover, so those who interact with gifted teens and children are encouraged to watch for negative changes in emotional state which last longer than a few weeks, and to trust their intuition if depression is suspected.

## Strategies to Consider

Please remember that I'm not a mental health professional, nor do I mean to gainsay the advice of those professionals.

However, if we view depression as an imbalance between pain and coping ability, then logically, in order to tackle the disorder, we must increase the coping mechanisms available to people, reduce the pain they are feeling, or both. You may even wish to have your child draw a balance scale and to label the items in each pan, so that he or she can begin to recognize and internalize the balance you are trying to help him or her to regain.

Sometimes, the number and intensity of the items on the *Things that Cause Pain* side of your child's balance can be overwhelming, but please don't let yourself feel so beleaguered that you don't begin to tackle them. You don't necessarily have to begin by confronting the largest issues, because making *any* progress on reducing your child's distress should bring him or her closer to being back in balance. In addition, we've already discussed some things that commonly cause distress in gifted children, and you have things you may be able to do to help fix these problems. Also, it's not uncommon that just knowing you have a plan to bring your child back to balance can alleviate some of your child's hopelessness – as well as your own – and they may be quite willing to work with you to address the items on the list.

## Depression

There are many tools and techniques which can become *Things That Help Me Deal with Pain*, as well. Obviously, if your child does not yet have the support of a therapist or counselor, you may wish to find one. Having someone else to talk with and learn other coping tools from can be invaluable, but don't be surprised if your child needs to try several individuals to get a good interpersonal fit. Not all therapists understand giftedness or gifted children, and being repeatedly misunderstood may well make your child feel worse. Don't be afraid to switch therapists if your child doesn't seem comfortable in the relationship.

There are a number of other tools you may try, as well. If your children suffer from depression stemming from global overwhelm, you might help them find relief by becoming active in nonprofit organizations which address their personal concerns, from rain forest preservation to feeding the hungry. If they counter that their actions can't actually solve the issue, you may wish to remind them that many people take comfort in the mantra, "Think globally, act locally," or, if you haven't already, tell them the story of the starfish[1]. "I made a difference to that one!" can be a powerful belief for children who want to help.

---

[1] There was a great storm over the ocean one night, and the following morning, *{make the hero of the story resemble your child}* walked onto the beach to find hundreds of starfish had been washed ashore by the storm. The child immediately began to pick up the starfish and throw them back into the water. An older gentleman walked up and asked, "Why are you wasting your time? There are hundreds of starfish here on the beach! You can't make a difference here." The child picked up another starfish, tossed it back into the sea, and said, "I made a difference to that one!" And *{he/ she}* continued down the beach.

If your children suffer from existential depression, that's admittedly a tough one. It's crucial that you hear their fears and concerns, without increasing them, if possible, but the very nature of existential crises is that these questions of existence do not have satisfactory answers. No one knows for sure what happens when we die, and we each give meaning to our lives as best we can. Thus, you may not be able to give your children answers that satisfy them. Many parents report that distraction is a helpful tool; signing your children up for a wide variety of new activities can force them to focus on what's happening in front of them rather than worrying about things over which they have no control. You may also wish to pay attention to Chapter Ten, as some of the ideas for dealing with anxiety may benefit your family.

## EFT to Help

Although EFT alone won't necessarily alleviate clinical depression, it can be a valuable tool in the effort to address the condition, because tapping works on both sides of our hypothetical balance.

The first way that EFT can benefit people with depression is purely by being an additional tool for coping with pain. Simply learning to use the tool gives depressed individuals another mechanism for dealing with painful emotions, and every additional coping tool that depressed children have at their disposal is another step toward regaining balance between the presence of pain and their ability to handle it.

If you choose to have your child work with an EFT practitioner, you may wish to list having the support of that individual as another item on the *Things That Help Me Deal with Pain* side of the balance. Knowing that there are people who have our backs when things are tough can be among the most important and valuable things to help us cope.

Tapping can also benefit people with depression by directly removing things from the *Things that Cause Pain* side of the scale. EFT was primarily created to release negative emotions, so it can remove the traumatic memories, issues, and fears that weigh down the Cause Pain side of the scale, one by one. Over time, tapping can significantly reduce the amount of distress people are responding to, helping bring pain and coping ability back into balance.

One tool that's commonly used in the EFT world is called the Personal Peace Procedure. This technique asks you or your children to create a list of all the events you can remember that hurt when they happened and still hurt now to recall. To be complete, you may wish to go through things methodically. Think of events related to each of the people you lived with as a child: your parents, your siblings, other people, even pets. From there, think of the important people outside your home, like neighbors or extended family members. Once you cover those key individuals, most people move through each school year sequentially, and for adults, you should consider your various jobs in turn. Remember to include important adult relationships, and finish with the people who live in your house today. In each case, you're looking for painful memories tied to things other people did to you, for example, when your father yelled at you for breaking the window; for painful memories tied to things you did to those other people, such as the guilt you still feel for hitting your brother with a rock; and also for painful events that you witnessed but weren't directly a party to, such as when your dog died.

Once the list has been created, tap through the memories, one each day, using the technique discussed in Chapter Three, until you've cleared them all. There is no hurry and no agenda, but gradually clearing out these painful memories over time should definitely help to reduce the sense that negative experiences outweigh your, or your children's, abilities to deal with them. Indeed, in an ideal world, undertaking this exercise will bring you and your children deep personal peace.

In addition to using EFT in a variety of long term ways to bring pain and coping ability back into balance, tapping can also be used to counter the feelings of being out of balance in the immediate term. This first script is designed to address the feeling of being overwhelmed that develops when your child has too few resources to deal with events in his or her life. As with all the scripts provided, it is intended to be simply a starting point for your family. Use your own words, add thoughts as they arise, and spend more time on certain phrases if they resonate for your children.

## Depression

| Point | Statement |
|---|---|
| *Karate chop* | Even though I feel like I can't handle my pain anymore, I'm trying to accept who I am and how I feel.<br><br>Even though I feel like I just can't take much more, I'm trying to be kind to myself.<br><br>Even though I feel overwhelmed by so much pain, so many things that have gone wrong... I want to love myself anyhow, even though it's really hard right now. |
| *Above the eye* | I feel so overwhelmed. |
| *Side of the eye* | So many things have gone wrong, |
| *Under the eye* | And I don't feel able to handle them all. |
| *Under the nose* | Some days, it feels like I'm drowning in all the awfulness. |
| *Under the mouth* | It feels like I can't catch my breath. |
| *Collarbone* | There are so many things wrong, and I can't actually fix any of them! |
| *Under the arm* | I sometimes feel scared and frustrated and helpless, |
| *Top of the head* | Because there are just so many problems I can't solve. |
| *Above the eye* | But I don't have to solve all the problems I see. |
| *Side of the eye* | It's not up to me to solve everyone's problems. |
| *Under the eye* | It's not even up to me to solve all MY problems right now. |

| Point | Statement |
| --- | --- |
| Under the nose | I don't have to have all the answers. |
| Under the mouth | It's okay to keep going without knowing how I'm going to resolve my issues. |
| Collarbone | I have time to figure things out, |
| Under the arm | Even if I'd really rather have everything fixed today! |
| Top of the head | But I don't have to have the answers today. |
| Above the eye | I'm allowed to figure things out over time. |
| Side of the eye | So for now, I allow myself to release my fear. |
| Under the eye | I allow myself to release my frustration. |
| Under the nose | I allow myself to release my helplessness. |
| Under the mouth | I allow myself to release my pain. |
| Collarbone | I can always go back to feeling those things in the future, if I want to… |
| Under the arm | But for now, I really don't want to! |
| Top of the head | I want to feel peace. |
| Above the eye | I want to feel safe. |
| Side of the eye | I want to know I can handle my pain. |
| Under the eye | And even though it may not always feel that way, I'm stronger than I know. |
| Under the nose | I am resilient. |
| Under the mouth | I have people who love me, and resources to help me. |
| Collarbone | I don't have to let the overwhelmed feelings win. |
| Under the arm | I can allow myself to relax and be all right. |

| Point | Statement |
|---|---|
| Top of the head | I can allow myself to feel safe right now. |
| Above the eye | I'm letting go of any remaining negative emotions. |
| Side of the eye | I release all remaining fear and frustration and helplessness and pain |
| Under the eye | From every fiber of my being, |
| Under the nose | And all the way back through my past. |
| Under the mouth | I allow myself to feel strong enough to handle whatever comes. |
| Collarbone | I choose to know I can handle the pains and disappointments that come my way. |
| Under the arm | I'm going to be okay. |
| Top of the head | And so it is. |
| *Take a deep breath in through your nose...* *Hold it for a few seconds...* *Release it slowly through your mouth.* | |

Although the emotional aspects of the disorder generally garner the most attention, depression is also an illness with physical components. The physical pains which accompany the disease – most commonly headaches and stomachaches in children – are very real and genuinely painful, and they should not be dismissed.

Luckily, EFT has the ability to reduce physical as well as emotional pain. It is believed that tapping works to relieve physical pain because pain is often a physical manifestation of emotional distress. However, you don't need to focus on the emotional aspects of the pain to experience relief. Simply tapping while talking about the symptoms frequently brings a reprieve.

When tapping on physical discomfort, as when tapping on a memory, you'll want to make sure you address as many aspects of the physical sensation as you can, because unaddressed aspects may not be fully resolved by the process. Describe the exact location of the pain, its intensity, and the nature of the pain, such as burning or aching, sharp or tingling. You may even wish to consider whether the sensation includes aspects such as color, shape, size, or movement, and if you find these are present, mention them while you work. As you know, the more detail you include in your tapping, the more effective it is.

Be aware that it's common when tapping on physical symptoms to experience what is called in the EFT world, "chasing the pain." After a few rounds of tapping on a symptom, your pain may seem to change or to move to another area of the body. In reality, what has happened is that you've eliminated the first pain and allowed a separate one to surface, but this is a good thing, because eliminating the first pain means that you've released the emotions it represented. As you continue to tap on each symptom in turn, you release the emotional distress which underlies each physical symptom, and this often allows you to clear a great deal of emotional upset without ever dealing directly with the emotions in play.

*Depression*

Also, note that tapping on physical pain may require some common-sense adaptations to the process of EFT. If your child is dealing with a headache, for example, you may not wish to have him or her knock repeatedly on his or her head. Instead, you may wish to gently massage some points rather than tapping them, or you may wish to contact an EFT practitioner for a list of alternative points you can use instead. EFT certainly isn't meant to contribute to discomfort!

One last common sense warning: if your child experiences recurrent physical pain, please have it checked by a doctor to rule out other causes.

This next script, designed to relieve a headache, can be adapted for use with all types of physical discomfort. It may seem odd to speak to directly to your, or your child's pain, but it works surprisingly well, so I encourage you to give it a try. As strange and as unlikely as it sounds, there are times when people feel like they get messages from physical sensations, so pay attention to whatever emotions or memories surface as you go through this script. There may be other things to address when this session is done.

Of course, you can do more than one round if the pain remains after the first pass through, but it's surprising how often there's a change in physical discomfort after only a short round of tapping. If you do decide to do a second round, you may get better results if you change the setup phrase to target, "This *remaining* pain in my forehead," rather than reusing the initial setup statement.

| Point | Statement |
|---|---|
| Karate chop | Even though I have a sharp pain in the middle of my forehead, I love and accept myself.<br><br>Even though I have this sharp pain in the middle of my forehead, I love and honor myself.<br><br>Even though my head is really hurting, I deeply and completely love, accept, and forgive myself. |
| Above the eye | This sharp pain in the middle of my forehead. |
| Side of the eye | I have a sharp, spiky pain in the middle of my forehead. |
| Under the eye | This stabbing, sharp pain right in the middle of my forehead. |
| Under the nose | It really hurts, but I want to let it go now. |
| Under the mouth | So I'm open to anything this pain wants me to hear. |
| Collarbone | I'm open to whatever I'm supposed to learn from this pain. |
| Under the arm | I'm hearing what it has to tell me, so that it can go away. |
| Top of the head | This sharp pain in my forehead has done its job. |
| Above the eye | It has gotten my attention, |
| Side of the eye | And conveyed whatever it needed to convey. |
| Under the eye | So I'm letting it go now. |
| Under the nose | I'm releasing all my pain. |
| Under the mouth | Physical, emotional, or spiritual. |

*Depression*

| Point | Statement |
|---|---|
| *Collarbone* | I'm letting go of all my discomfort now. |
| *Under the arm* | Releasing any remaining pain in my forehead, |
| *Top of the head* | So I can enjoy peace and comfort. |
| *Take a deep breath in through your nose...* | |
| *Hold it for a few seconds...* | |
| *Release it slowly through your mouth.* | |

Up to this point, we've been creating scripts for use by a person suffering from depression, but we all know that the disorder cuts a wide swath of destruction. The family and friends of a person with depression suffer as well, because it hurts to watch someone we love being destroyed by the illness, while we are forced to stand by, unable to do nearly as much as we'd like to help.

The pain endured by the family and friends of depressed individuals is very real. If one of your loved ones is depressed, you probably experience guilt, fear, frustration, worry, and hurt, among other things, along with a strong desire to help which you cannot actually satisfy. It's a terrible position to be in.

The last script in this chapter has been created specifically for those who care about individuals with depression. It is for you to tap through yourself. I hope it brings you comfort.

*Tapping for the Gifted Child*

| Point | Statement |
|---|---|
| Karate chop | Even though it hurts to watch {name of person} struggle with depression, I completely accept my feelings right now.<br><br>Even though I feel kind of weird worrying about my pain when {name of person} is dealing with so much worse, I accept myself and how I feel.<br><br>Even though it is so hard to watch {name of person} struggle with depression, I love, accept, and forgive myself today. |
| Above the eye | {Name of person} is struggling with depression, |
| Side of the eye | And I feel almost silly worrying about how I feel, when that depression is so much worse than what I'm dealing with. |
| Under the eye | But the fact is, it's hard to watch {him/her} suffer this way. |
| Under the nose | It hurts so much to watch {him/her} hurting. |
| Under the mouth | And I'm so scared. |
| Collarbone | I'm afraid {he/she} won't get better. |
| Under the arm | And what if {he/she} gets worse?! |
| Top of the head | What will I do then? |
| Above the eye | I feel so helpless. |
| Side of the eye | I want so much to help {him/her} get better! |
| Under the eye | I want {him/her} to be well! |
| Under the nose | But I can't make that happen, |

*Depression*

| Point | Statement |
|---|---|
| Under the mouth | And it makes me so sad to know this. |
| Collarbone | It's hard to see {him/ her} suffer and not be able to do as much as I would like to, to help. |
| Under the arm | Sometimes I feel guilty. |
| Top of the head | I feel like I really should be doing more. |
| Above the eye | And sometimes I feel really angry! |
| Side of the eye | Angry at myself, for not being able to make a difference! |
| Under the eye | And angry at {him/ her} for not being able to just feel better. |
| Under the nose | But that makes me feel guilty again, because I know {he/ she} isn't depressed on purpose. |
| Under the mouth | It's an illness. |
| Collarbone | And I would give just about anything to help {him/ her} recover, |
| Under the arm | But there's only so much I can do. |
| Top of the head | So at other times, I'm afraid. |
| Above the eye | I'm scared that things may get worse. |
| Side of the eye | I'm afraid {he/ she} may do something drastic, |
| Under the eye | And that is terrifying! |
| Under the nose | I just wish {he/ she} would get better. |
| Under the mouth | I want {him/ her} to be like {he/ she} was before. |
| Collarbone | I want {him/ her} to laugh. |
| Under the arm | And be happy. |
| Top of the head | And be safe. |

| Point | Statement |
|---|---|
| Above the eye | And I can't make those things happen, |
| Side of the eye | But it's okay for me to wish for them. |
| Under the eye | It's natural for people to want these things for their loved ones. |
| Under the nose | Everyone who has ever loved a person with depression has had these same wishes, |
| Under the mouth | And these same fears, |
| Collarbone | And these same guilts, |
| Under the arm | And been angry about the same things. |
| Top of the head | It's hard for anyone to watch someone they love suffer in this way. |
| Above the eye | I'm not alone. |
| Side of the eye | And if my pain gets to be too much for me, I can reach out for help, too. |
| Under the eye | That doesn't make me weak, |
| Under the nose | And it doesn't take anything away from what {name of person} is dealing with. |
| Under the mouth | But I deserve to be taken care of, too. |
| Collarbone | {His/her} suffering is causing me to suffer, but I don't have to suffer endlessly. |
| Under the arm | I can choose to take care of myself. |
| Top of the head | And that doesn't make me selfish! |
| Above the eye | It's okay for me to be compassionate toward myself. |

## Depression

| Point | Statement |
|---|---|
| Side of the eye | It's okay for me to behave in a loving way toward myself. |
| Under the eye | Because I count, too, and my needs are important. |
| Under the nose | And another thing I can do for myself |
| Under the mouth | Is to stop worrying quite so much about {name of person}. |
| Collarbone | I would never abandon {him/ her}! |
| Under the arm | But if worry were going to help {him/ her} get better, it would have done so already. |
| Top of the head | My worry isn't helping {him/ her}, and it's not helping me. |
| Above the eye | I'm making myself downright sick at times with worry, |
| Side of the eye | And that doesn't help anyone at all. |
| Under the eye | So I'm choosing to let go of some of my worry. |
| Under the nose | I'm going to let go of some of my fear. |
| Under the mouth | I'm going to release my anger. |
| Collarbone | I'm letting go of my guilt. |
| Under the arm | It's time to release these negative emotions. |
| Top of the head | It's also time to stop punishing myself for anything I imagine I may have done to contribute to {name of person}'s condition. |
| Above the eye | It's time to forgive myself, |
| Side of the eye | And it's time to forgive {name of person}, too. |

| Point | Statement |
|---|---|
| Under the eye | {He/she} doesn't want me to suffer on {his/her} behalf. |
| Under the nose | It's just what happens when you love someone. |
| Under the mouth | And I do love {name of person} and I want {him/her} to get well. |
| Collarbone | But {his/her} health isn't in my hands. |
| Under the arm | Just like {his/her} journey isn't up to me. |
| Top of the head | {Name of person} came here to fulfill {his/her} own life's purpose. |
| Above the eye | I don't know how depression fits in to that. I may never know. |
| Side of the eye | But I'm letting go now of my desire for control, because I cannot control the outcome. |
| Under the eye | I can and will do all I can to support {him/her}, |
| Under the nose | But I'm finally acknowledging that this condition is not in my control. |
| Under the mouth | It's time to release my need to control things. |
| Collarbone | I will handle whatever comes. |
| Under the arm | I will support {name of person} to the best of my ability, |
| Top of the head | And trust the rest to {God/the Universe, etc}. |
| Take a deep breath in through your nose... | |
| Hold it for a few seconds... | |
| Release it slowly through your mouth. | |

CHAPTER TEN

# Anxiety

Megan had taken great pains to explain their upcoming road trip to her five year old daughter, Chloe. Chloe was easily upset by anything unanticipated, so she had explained how long the drive would take, where they would stay, and what they would eat. She'd been careful to pack Chloe's pillow and blanket and favorite stuffed animals. She'd done everything possible to set Chloe's mind at ease before they left home.

The long drive was, thankfully, uneventful, although Chloe seemed not to breathe as they drove between the high rises of the unfamiliar downtown. Megan pointed out their hotel so Chloe would see that they were close to their destination and was relieved to hear Chloe take her first deep breath in nearly half an hour.

Their GPS unit instructed them to turn the wrong way down a one-way street to get to the entrance to the parking garage, so Megan prepared to drive around the block. Not ten feet past the one-way street, a panic-stricken little voice piped up from the back seat, "Oh great, Mommy! Now we're lost!" And Chloe burst into tears.

Megan felt both frustrated and despairing. She'd done everything right in planning this trip, but *still* she had a hysterical kindergartner literally in view of their final destination. There was nothing for Chloe to be afraid of! Why was everything with this child so *hard?*

Like depression, anxiety is recognized as an emotional disorder by the conventional medical community. Many people have worked with conventional practitioners to find relief from their anxiety, and if the anxiety experienced by you or your children is severe, traditional medications and therapies are available. However, there also exist many less conventional therapies which also bring relief to people who suffer from anxiety, including EFT. Tapping can help people to feel less controlled by their fears. In mild cases, it can often be used instead of standard techniques to eliminate emotional disquiet; in cases of severe anxiety, it can safely be used in conjunction with traditional approaches to reduce overall levels of discomfort.

According to the US National Institutes of Health, 18% of adults in the US have been formally diagnosed with an anxiety disorder. (National Institutes of Health, 2015) Studies of gifted children draw conflicting conclusions on whether giftedness increases the likelihood that an individual will experience major anxiety (Neihart, The Impact of Giftedness on Psychological Well-Being, 1999), but even if gifted people only experience anxiety at the same rate as the general population, that means that nearly one gifted person in five will experience significant anxiety for some measurable portion of their lives.

Most behaviors exist on a continuum, and anxiety is no different. The experience ranges from mild, localized anxiousness driven by things like performing in public or visiting the doctor, all the way up to phobias and formal anxiety disorders, of which generalized anxiety disorder, panic disorder, and social anxiety disorder are the most common. The more severe the level of anxiety, the more disruptive and potentially dangerous it is, but even mild anxiety can affect the quality of life of the person who suffers from it, as well as the people in his or her life.

It's easy to see how gifted individuals may be prone to feeling anxiety. Their sensitivity makes them extremely alert to even small changes in their environment, which may trigger the common human response of considering unfamiliar things, potentially threatening. Their sometimes-extreme sensitivity to environmental stimuli may also make them go through life on edge, fearfully anticipating the next loud noise or intolerable smell. Their emotional intensity may make ordinary situations seem overwhelming – more scary, or more uncontrollable – and they may therefore feel unsafe in situations when neurotypical individuals do not.

Anxiety is a component of many other experiences that are common to gifted individuals. Perfectionism, for example, is really an ongoing state of anxiety driven by a fear of failure. Imposter syndrome involves constant fear and worry about being found out as a fraud. The isolation that arises when gifted children endure a poor social fit may result in those children learning an anxious response to social situations, potentially ultimately creating some form of social anxiety disorder. Twice exceptionality can give rise to nearly constant fear of being unable to perform at the required level. Many aspects of the gifted experience include some level of fear and anxiety.

Note that in certain circumstances, anxiety may be a result of psychological triggering of negative past events for both gifted and non-gifted individuals. For example, if your child has a negative experience with a dog, future experiences with dogs may trigger the previous negative experience, and this may manifest as anxiety around, or even a phobia, of dogs.

## What It Looks Like

Worry is the hallmark of all forms of anxiety, and some children simply have a more worried temperament than others. Their worry may not qualify them for formal diagnoses of anxiety disorders, but their endless concerns take a toll on their health, and sometimes on the patience of the people around them when they seem to see endless danger where there is none.

Our brains and bodies are designed to respond immediately to danger, even if those threats aren't apparent to anyone else. Thus, children with anxiety frequently experience physical symptoms that are a part of the fight or flight response, because their bodies are preparing to respond to whatever imminent disaster they think is coming. In the most severe circumstances, they may experience a racing heart or shortness of breath, as their bodies prepare to run away from a danger that may or may not be there. In less severe cases, they may display a somewhat jumpy demeanor as they constantly look around them for the source of the (imaged) danger, or they may fidget incessantly as their bodies work off some of their excess adrenalin.

Frequent fight or flight responses may also cause children to have physical pain. They may have spent the whole day shaking their legs or clenching their jaw without even being aware of it, and these muscles may become tired and achy. Your children may even be prone to getting colds and other illnesses, as their immune systems may become worn out by their bodies' constant vigilance against threats which never materialize.

Their heightened state of arousal makes it very difficult for children with anxiety to relax, even in places where their parents believe they are safe. You may notice your child is simply unable to let his or her guard down and seems always on edge, even at home. The inability to relax can affect your child's ability to sleep, as well. In fact, insomnia is one of the diagnostic criteria for full-blown anxiety disorders (DSM). If your child's worries keep him or her up at night, you're likely dealing with some form of anxiety.

## Strategies to Consider

I've mentioned before that I am not a medical professional. I do not mean to dispense medical advice, nor to counter the advice of medical professionals. If your child experiences severe anxiety, I encourage you to seek medical assistance in dealing with it, because the sooner you alleviate the condition, the better off your child will be (Akil, 2016). However, in addition to encouraging you to seek conventional support, I'm also going to mention a few therapies which are not widely discussed in conventional circles that have helped people I know to reduce their anxiety. Please do your own research prior to trying these and use your common sense in all cases.

The first thing I would suggest you investigate is the fact that feelings of anxiety are a common symptom of a dietary mineral deficiency. In particular, it is almost impossible for people to get the daily recommended amount of magnesium from diet alone, and most multi-vitamins don't supplement to the full recommended amount, either. Therefore, it's extremely common for people to be deficient in dietary magnesium, and one of the primary symptoms of deficiency is generalized anxiety. If you or your family members experience generalized anxiety, you may wish to consider adding an over-the-counter magnesium supplement to your family's diet. Many people prefer to work with the powdered form, as this allows you to precisely control the dose, but other forms may work, as well. You need to be careful not to overdose, as this will cause diarrhea, but all supplements will have dosing instructions on the package and can be picked up at any drug or health food store. Magnesium supplementation has been known to radically reduce the presence of anxiety for some individuals.

Persistent anxiety is also a common symptom of B vitamin deficiency, but there's a catch. While supplementing the diet with B vitamins may alleviate some cases of anxiety, many individuals possess mutations in certain genes which make it impossible for them to properly metabolize B vitamins. In order to overcome their vitamin deficits, they may need to take very specific types of these vitamins, already in bio-available form. You may wish to research, and possibly test for, the MTHFR genetic mutation if you feel your children's anxiety simply hasn't responded to other treatments. If it turns out that members of your family have this mutation, simple dietary supplementation may bring vast relief.

Other widely available over-the-counter tools that may bring powerful relief to some people are flower essences. If you're not familiar with them, these remedies are commonly used in many parts of the world, bringing the energetic signatures of specific plants – and often a great deal of relief – to bear on people's distress. Each plant is used for a different purpose, such as aspen for unspecific fears, or pine for guilt. They don't eliminate the emotional issue you're dealing with, so much as make it easier to tolerate, and this gentle action can be very comforting for many people. Flower essences aren't conventional drugs, which means they don't work through conventional means, nor have they endured standard tests of efficacy; however, I know a number of people who swear by the results they get from flower essences, so you may wish to do some research of your own on these therapies. Fear and anxiety seem to respond particularly well to flower essences.

## EFT to Help

When we turn our attention to EFT, tapping can help to release the negative emotions which accompany anxiety, including feeling overwhelmed, unsafe, or fearful. Back in Chapter Two, we talked about a standard, three-step formula you can use when tapping with your children to release their negative emotions. Specifically, you want to name and acknowledge the current emotion as precisely as you can, using detailed descriptors and synonyms, if appropriate; you then want to validate the emotion, reminding the person that their feelings are normal, allowed, and even common; and then you want to guide the person to let the emotion go because it isn't needed any longer. As a rule, this formula works well for virtually all negative emotions, but you need to be a little careful about following it too closely with anxiety and fear.

When validating a person's current emotional state, it's common to emphasize how very normal their response is to whatever situation they're experiencing. We might encourage them to say things like, "Anyone would feel this way in my shoes," or "Of course I feel this way!" However, when dealing with fears, and particularly when working with people for whom anxiety is a concern, we may wish to downplay how common their response is. While it can be comforting to hear of our sadness, "Anyone would feel sad in this situation!" it is generally less reassuring to be told, "Anyone would be afraid in this

*Anxiety*

situation!" Words like this simply give our fears more legitimacy and make them harder, rather than easier, to release.

Instead, when using EFT on fear, it is usually more helpful to state that the person tapping has valid feelings, without emphasizing that the fear itself is common and reasonable. For example, rather than saying, "Of course I'm afraid. Anyone would be!" it may be more helpful to say, "How I feel is valid, and I'm allowed to feel this way if I want to. But I don't want to!" From here, you can move directly into releasing the fear. This lets your child know that his or her emotions are okay, no matter what they are, but that some feelings are better let go because they don't particularly serve us.

In addition to using EFT to release negative emotions, remember that you can use the techniques discussed in Chapter Three if your child's anxiety is due to psychological triggering of past negative events. Tapping through the painful memories which keep being called to the surface means they won't be an issue going forward, and this should lessen your child's anxiousness overall.

It's important to note that the fears which arise in people with anxiety are frequently irrational, and therefore, they cannot be rationalized away. You may wish to remind your children that they are safe and things will be fine, but often, anxious children will simply counter your every attempt to reassure them with a, "But what about *this*?" response. They will ask about every possibility. How will you keep them safe if you are at work? What if they've got the flu when {something} happens? Their brains are simply too good at finding potentially dangerous loopholes in every situation for you to ever fully calm their fears.

Since it's often impossible to reduce the number or even the intensity of your child's fears, often the best thing you can do is to use EFT to increase their confidence in their ability to cope with whatever happens. As noted in Chapter Seven, tapping can be extremely valuable when addressing fears of all kinds. We can use tapping to acknowledge our surface fear, we can allow ourselves to admit our deeper fear of being unable to handle the situation if or when it arises, we can release the fear, and then we can replace it with confidence in our ability to deal with whatever life brings. The following script uses this formula to release an undisclosed fear, but you can adjust it to reflect the specific worries your child faces.

| Point | Statement |
| --- | --- |
| *Karate chop* | Even though I'm afraid of {this}, I accept myself and all my feelings. |
|  | Even though I feel afraid of {this}, I am trying to love and accept myself as I am. |
|  | Even though I feel afraid of {this} and I hate being afraid, I'm trying very hard to accept how I feel in this moment. |
| *Above the eye* | I'm afraid. |

## Anxiety

| Point | Statement |
|---|---|
| *Side of the eye* | I feel so scared. |
| *Under the eye* | {This} may happen. |
| *Under the nose* | I can't stop it from happening, and that makes me feel helpless. |
| *Under the mouth* | And feeling helpless makes me feel more afraid, |
| *Collarbone* | And I just can't handle it! |
| *Under the arm* | That's what I'm afraid of most of all. |
| *Top of the head* | I'm afraid I can't handle it if {this} happens. |
| *Above the eye* | And I hate feeling this way! |
| *Side of the eye* | I'm allowed to feel this way, but I sure don't like it. |
| *Under the eye* | So I'm going to let my fear go. |
| *Under the nose* | My fear isn't serving me in any way, |
| *Under the mouth* | So I'm releasing it now. |
| *Collarbone* | I'm letting go of all my fear. |
| *Under the arm* | Releasing it from every cell in my body, |
| *Top of the head* | And all the way back through my past. |
| *Above the eye* | I don't need to feel afraid, |
| *Side of the eye* | Because I am strong and capable. |
| *Under the eye* | I have people to help and support me. |
| *Under the nose* | And I am able to handle whatever happens in my life! |
| *Under the mouth* | So there's no reason for me to be afraid. |
| *Collarbone* | Even if I sometimes have to deal with challenging events, |

| Point | Statement |
|---|---|
| Under the arm | I know I can do it. |
| Top of the head | I've got this! |
| Take a deep breath in through your nose... Hold it for a few seconds... Release it slowly through your mouth. | |

Also, particularly if your child experiences mild or infrequent anxiety, the following routine about safety may be helpful.

| Point | Statement |
|---|---|
| Karate chop | Even though I don't feel safe right now, I accept myself and all my feelings. |
| | Even though I don't feel at all safe right now, I love and accept myself fully. |
| | Even though I feel frightened and unsafe, I deeply and completely love and accept all parts of myself, even my fear. |
| Above the eye | I feel unsafe. |
| Side of the eye | I feel afraid. |
| Under the eye | It's so hard for me to just relax and feel safe. |
| Under the nose | I'm constantly afraid something bad is going to happen. |

| Point | Statement |
|---|---|
| *Under the mouth* | I'm not even sure what it is, but I'm sure something bad is going to happen. |
| *Collarbone* | And this means my system is on constant alert. |
| *Under the arm* | My body and mind are constantly trying to protect me from danger. |
| *Top of the head* | And I thank them for working so hard to keep me safe. |
| *Above the eye* | I'm grateful that they try so hard to protect me. |
| *Side of the eye* | But I'm letting them know that they can relax now. |
| *Under the eye* | I'm not actually in any danger. |
| *Under the nose* | I am safe right now. |
| *Under the mouth* | I can't control everything that happens in the world, |
| *Collarbone* | But I know I can handle whatever comes my way. |
| *Under the arm* | I am strong and brave and resilient. |
| *Top of the head* | I can deal with whatever comes. |
| *Above the eye* | And that is good to know, in case something bad happens. |
| *Side of the eye* | But there is no reason to believe a bad thing will happen right now. |
| *Under the eye* | I am safe. |
| *Under the nose* | So I'm letting go of all my fear. |
| *Under the mouth* | I'm letting go of all my worry. |
| *Collarbone* | I'm remembering that I and my loved ones are okay. |

*Tapping for the Gifted Child*

| Point | Statement |
|---|---|
| *Under the arm* | I'm letting go of all my worries, |
| *Top of the head* | Because I am safe and I'm going to be okay. |
| *Take a deep breath in through your nose...* ||
| *Hold it for a few seconds...* ||
| *Release it slowly through your mouth.* ||

CHAPTER ELEVEN

# Positive Disintegration

Annabeth's parents stared at her closed bedroom door. The sound of sobbing could be heard coming from behind it, and they wanted to go to her and comfort her in some way but were at a loss about what to say. Every time they had gone into her room when she cried the past few months, she had flown into a rage at their interruption.

Annabeth's crying fits had become more frequent of late, nearly daily events. They often seemed to be precipitated by one of the many self-help books she picked up at the library, or by one of the endless series of self-development podcasts she listened to. But when her parents asked if perhaps Annabeth might wish to speak to someone – a counselor, perhaps – about her continuous crying, she had snapped at them.

"I don't want to see a *counselor*," she said. "They would just want to *fix* me!"

Now her parents stared once again at the door which separated them from their crying daughter and wondered what to do. Of course, they would go in, but what then? How were they supposed to actually help her?

■    ■    ■

During the 1960's and 1970's, Polish psychologist Kazimierz Dabrowski developed a robust and complex theory of personality development which he called the Theory of Positive Disintegration. The details of his theory are too numerous and nuanced for this discussion, but there are aspects of his theory that resonate very deeply with some members of the gifted community, so I'd like to touch on them briefly in case this helps your family at some point.

According to Dabrowski, some individuals will, at various points in their lives, prune what they see as negative trait and behaviors from their personalities in order to make room to expand their more generous and compassionate natures. The process is called disintegration, because the person must, to some degree, take apart their existing personality in order to extract the behaviors they no longer want. He considered it *positive* disintegration because he believed that the end result of this development work would ultimately be a stronger, healthier individual, although the process itself may not feel positive as one is going through it.

Dabrowski believed that only some people have the ability to undertake this pruning. He believed that the chance to develop what he called an advanced personality was due to a combination of inborn characteristics which he called high development potential. In particular, people with high development potential have special talents, such as athletic or musical abilities; a strong drive to express themselves, which he called the "third factor;" and overexcitabilities, which are increased sensitivity in the nervous system to various stimuli (Tillier, 1995).

Although Dabrowski wasn't deliberately writing about gifted individuals, he described five overexcitabilities, sometimes shortened to OEs, which many people in the gifted community feel accurately depict much of the experience of gifted children and adults (Lind, 2001). His five overexcitabilities are:

1. *Intellectual Overexcitability* is a need to gain knowledge and seek understanding. Individuals with intellectual overexcitability ask difficult questions, dig deeply into topics which interest them, move quickly through material, and draw novel connections between ideas.

2. *Sensual Overexcitability* is a heightened experience of the five senses, which may be pleasant or unpleasant. Individuals with sensual overexcitability may get more pleasure than most from listening to music or eating fine foods, but they may also be overwhelmed by sounds, smells, or tastes.

3. *Imaginational Overexcitability* is a powerful experience of the imagination. Individuals with imaginational overexcitability are often extremely creative and enjoy creating art, writing stories, and daydreaming.

4. *Psychomotor Overexcitability* is a capacity for activity and movement. Individuals with psychomotor overexcitability love to move, hate

to wait, and often seem to have more energy than they know what to do with.

5. *Emotional Overexcitability* is a heightened emotional response to pretty much everything. Individuals with emotional overexcitability are often accused of being overly dramatic or of overreacting to things, because they feel, and often express, very deep emotions, even to relatively small stimuli.

Although these overexcitabilities frequently resonate with gifted individuals and researchers, OEs are only a small sliver of the Theory of Positive Disintegration. As noted, Dabrowski considered these to be some of the inborn characteristics of individuals who had high developmental potential, but not all individuals who possess OEs will go on to exhibit advanced personality development. Thus, the central question of Dabrowski's work focused on figuring out who, how, and why some people live lives of astounding compassion and moral upstanding, while others do not.

According to him, some individuals with high developmental potential will choose to do the work of removing what they believe to be their negative instincts from their personalities and aligning their behavior with their more generous and compassionate tendencies. They do this, not by building those advanced personality traits on top of earlier behaviors, but by fully dismantling and replacing their less advanced traits.

According to Dabrowski, this dismantling process looks a great deal like mental illness, but it should be viewed as a positive development, because it means the person is choosing to move to a more advanced state of development (Mowrer, 1965). Inner conflict between the person you are and the person you feel you should be can spark negative emotions such as guilt, anxiety, or shame, and these emotions, in turn, can propel you into higher levels of personality development. These negative emotions are an essential part of positive disintegration, and therefore, shouldn't necessarily be "fixed." As you might imagine, Dabrowski's positive disintegration is an emotionally painful process, although it results, ultimately, in psychological reintegration at a higher level of human functioning.

Given that Dabrowski's OEs are possible indicators of positive disintegration, and given that they so closely describe many aspects of the gifted experience, one would expect it to be fairly common for gifted individuals to experience positive disintegration, and there are many anecdotal reports of this happening. However, research hasn't yet been done to establish the frequency of positive disintegration events in the gifted population.

### What It Looks Like

Positive disintegration can happen at any age. Within the general population, it's common during adolescence and midlife; among gifted individuals, positive disintegration may happen many times, at any age, as individuals move through the stages of development. Positive disintegration may be initiated by external forces such as changing schools or jobs, or the end of a major relationship; however, after its initial phase, it becomes something the person continues voluntarily, not necessarily because they want to, but because they feel compelled to. They feel they are growing in essential and beneficial ways and work hard to continue that growth.

What makes the experience of positive disintegration difficult to describe is that, quite frankly, it tends to look a lot like the experience of depression. It may involve low mood, irritability, and a tendency to question one's worth and contributions. It may also contain aspects of anxiety, perfectionism, and isolation. It can be extremely difficult to distinguish positive disintegration from these other phenomena.

However, in conversations with people who are undergoing positive disintegration, a common theme that will come up is that they *don't want help*. Granted, sometimes people with depression won't want help, either; they're apathetic or despairing about professional help actually making a difference in their lives. People going through positive disintegration, however, will often disdain the "supposed assistance" of therapists or counselors, who commonly see their state as something to be fixed rather than something to be learned from. At other times, people experiencing positive disintegration may feel that they're supposed to face and conquer their problems alone. They may even describe it as a test to see if they're worthy of having the peace they seek.

People experiencing positive disintegration will often spontaneously undertake various forms of what Dabrowski called auto-therapy, exploring their own minds and temperaments to better understand themselves and to root out their own weaknesses. They may read extensively about self-development topics, take classes and workshops, or try a variety of self-help techniques, sometimes unconventional, ranging from meditation to drumming. And yes, this may include tapping.

Friends and families of people experiencing positive disintegration may find the process frustrating or even frightening. Watching your loved one suffer can be painful, and positive disintegration definitely includes suffering. The process is also frequently protracted, as old beliefs and weaknesses are dismantled and new ones are created and integrated into the personality. Positive disintegration isn't pretty, and it's not fast, but for those who come through the process, it is utterly transformative. By the time the person has gone through the transformation, the entire personality has been shifted to something more integrated, whole, and healthy.

## Strategies to Consider

It can be a little tricky to offer support to people who believe that an important part of their journey is to accept little to no assistance.

One thing that you may be able to do is to listen and offer understanding. If your children tell you that they're growing or figuring out who they are, even if it looks to you like depression, you may wish to honor their experience. You may not wish to force them to go to therapy, for example, unless they cross some threshold that you and they agree to in advance, such as acting on any thoughts of self-harm.

You may also find it useful to talk to your kids about the idea of positive disintegration in general. You may be able to help them reframe what the world would tend to call their "neurotic symptoms" as creative and developmental tools. It may be comforting for them to be reminded that sometimes when it feels like things are falling apart, they're really falling into place.

You may also be able to support your children's growth by providing tools for developmental auto-therapy. You may encourage them to read widely or attend workshops related to self-development. You may wish to help them find the works of great teachers in a variety of fields and traditions, and you may particularly wish to support their exploration of ideas and world views with which you yourself are unfamiliar. Positive disintegration involves breaking down what doesn't serve your children's highest self and replacing it with what your kids consider more useful ideas, even if those ideas don't always make sense to their parents.

## EFT to Help

I'm not including a script in this chapter because positive disintegration is such a personal process. In many ways, perhaps the best thing you can do is to teach your children EFT and allow them to use it in whatever ways seem most appropriate to them. They may choose to root out limiting beliefs, to release their fears, or to heal the anger that holds them back. EFT won't allow your children to bypass the process of disintegration, but tapping can make it faster and more productive.

If necessary, don't forget to use EFT yourself. Trying to support your children through the process of positive disintegration can be difficult and exhausting, so if you need to release any negative emotions of your own, go ahead and tap them away. You can check out the end of Chapter Ten if you'd like to see a script you can modify for your use.

PART FOUR

# The Apple Doesn't Fall Far From the Tree

Whether we like to admit it or not, many of our children's characteristics come from their parents in some combination of nature and nurture, and giftedness is no exception. The fact that you're parenting a gifted child could well mean that you, yourself, were a gifted child, and it may be helpful to make your own peace with giftedness so you can better support your children.

CHAPTER TWELVE

# Parental Denial

Mitch hoped his mother would answer the phone, but she was so busy in retirement, he wasn't sure she would. She wasn't presently on one of her international trips, but she was taking tai chi and learning bridge and had joined not one but two book clubs, which meant she was often too busy to chat. She answered on the last ring, because she'd had to put down her paintbrushes. He had forgotten today was her painting class.

Mitch started to tell her about the recent testing that indicated his son was gifted. The information they'd been given about giftedness seemed to explain a lot of Mitch's quirks, as well, and Mitch wondered if his mother had ever noticed these traits in him.

"Oh, honey, you weren't gifted. You were never any smarter than anyone else in the neighborhood; you were just weird. You were always so intense, so sure you were right. To be fair, you often were! But you were so sensitive to what everyone said. You were always just like me – just like my father, in fact. But we're not gifted. We're just strange."

As she hung up to finish her painting, Mitch was more convinced than ever that he'd been gifted as a child, and probably she had been, as well. He wondered why she refused to see that there had been gifted children in their family for generations without anyone realizing it.

It's quite common for parents to be unaware of our own giftedness until we find ourselves navigating the gifted world with our children. It's true that we may have felt different from the other kids when we were young, or we may have participated in pullout programs in elementary school, but somehow, that seems so long ago. Plus, many areas now have programs that differ from what was available to us when we were children, making it seem like we're in a very different era. Our childhoods are ancient history. None of that can possibly have any bearing on our lives today.

Given this common perception, for many parents, entering the gifted world can be a revelation. We begin by learning how gifted individuals learn more quickly than their classmates, and how giftedness manifests in math or language abilities, in love of puns and puzzles. Hopefully, we also learn about other gifted traits like intensity, need for justice, and sensitivity, and how these traits reinforce one another and affect our lives, and suddenly, things make sense. We begin to understand, not only our children, but why we always felt like outsiders back when we were children, why we stood out in our classrooms, even why we were drawn to the people we were. Many of us begin to see ourselves as having been genuinely different and misunderstood, rather than the freaks we may have been accused of being. For many parents, confronting and accepting the fact that we, ourselves, were gifted children, can bring a great deal of relief.

Not only do we learn that we were gifted as children, but we often learn that we've grown up to become gifted adults. After all, giftedness doesn't go away when we age. Despite the claims of some school systems that "everyone evens out by third grade," this simply isn't true. It may be true that some precocious youngsters realize by third grade that they will never have their needs met in this setting, becoming despairing or angry or simply withdrawn, but that doesn't mean that these children are no longer gifted. It simply means their giftedness isn't being supported at this point. Stephanie Tolan makes this point beautifully in a marvelous essay entitled, "Is It a Cheetah?" If you haven't read it, you may wish to check it out. It's listed in the references section.

Other people may have their gifted needs met to one degree or another during childhood, but still, somehow the assumption is that giftedness doesn't apply to adulthood. In adulthood, people tend to equate eminence with giftedness, so high performers are seen as gifted while less prominent adults are often considered "ordinary." However, as you know, giftedness isn't just about output; it's about the differences in how one's brain works. Giftedness affects all aspects of life: how we see ourselves and the world, how we learn, how we think, how we feel emotionally and even, often, physically.

These inherent differences don't go away when we grow up. Gifted children become gifted adults.

Some parents are able to easily transition from the knowledge that they were gifted children, to the knowledge that they are currently gifted adults, but this step isn't a given. Many adults resist thinking of themselves as gifted for a variety of reasons.

In communities where giftedness isn't embraced, it can be hard for parents to own this aspect of themselves. There are many places where being gifted is seen as elitist, snobbish, or entitled, and there are many people who view gifted individuals as getting "too big for their britches." Parents quite naturally don't want to be painted with those brushes. Although they may be willing to fight for the needs of their children, they may deny that aspect of their own beings because it doesn't feel safe to admit to having those traits themselves. They may deny their own giftedness out of a sense of self-protection.

Even in communities where giftedness is not viewed with a hostile eye, there are many parents who deny their own abilities due to a need or desire to fit in. This may be especially common among parents who felt like outsiders as children, due to their giftedness or other factors, such as race, immigration status, economic circumstances, health status... the list is virtually endless. People who spent large portions of their childhoods feeling like outcasts may go to great lengths as adults to be seen as "normal," even if it means denying their intellectual abilities.

Other adults who deny that they're gifted may do so because they have a hard time even seeing their intellectual abilities due to the presence of learning disabilities. As discussed in Chapter Six, learning disabilities, especially ones which have been undiagnosed, may cause people to perform at a "normal" level and therefore assume they are "normal" people, not recognizing that their disabilities depress their level of output from where it would be if they were working in accordance with their gifted abilities. In fact, many people are unaware that twice exceptionality even exists, so when LDs prevent them from performing the way "gifted people do," they assume they cannot possibly be gifted. These parents don't realize that giftedness is about neurological differences, not about output.

Adults with imposter syndrome also often deny that they're gifted. As noted in Chapter Five, people with imposter syndrome will go to great lengths to avoid the cognitive dissonance that can arise from the disconnect between their self-concepts and their clear abilities in many areas. They generally ascribe their successes to factors outside themselves, such as being lucky or being in the right place at the right time. People who spend years giving credit for their successes to factors outside themselves will rarely spontaneously begin to own their abilities as adults. They often genuinely fail to recognize that their own superior abilities are what have allowed them to succeed through the years and will deny any giftedness in themselves throughout their lives.

Yet another common reason adults deny their giftedness is because they may have spent their lives surrounded by other gifted people. In Chapter Eight, we discussed how gifted individuals naturally gravitate to people of similar abilities. This often means that throughout their lives, no matter how accomplished they themselves were, many gifted individuals spent their time with equally talented relatives and friends. It may be almost impossible for them to see themselves as special because the people around them may have abilities which cause their own gifts to pale in comparison. What adults in these circumstances fail to recognize, however, is that giftedness, by definition, means working differently from neurotypical individuals. Just because you may have been raised in a family of gifted individuals, or spent your time with gifted friends, doesn't mean you are "normal." It just means your view of "normal" is skewed.

Parental denial of their own giftedness can stem from many sources, but its effects are far-reaching for parents and their children.

Parents who do not, or cannot, recognize their own giftedness often suffer without this understanding. Using giftedness as a lens to understand yourself can help to explain behaviors and traits that are completely natural to you, but which seem odd to the people around you. For example, knowing that you are gifted means you can see yourself as possessing the common gifted trait of being intense, rather than thinking of yourself as "high maintenance," and knowing that gifted individuals are often passionate about justice may explain some of your

*Parental Denial*

lifelong obsession with fairness. In the context of being gifted, many behaviors can be seen as par for the course, but without this understanding, they can be considered perplexing, troubling, or otherwise negative.

Parental denial of their own giftedness also sets a bad example for their children. When parents deny crucial aspects of themselves, the children watching them may learn to do the same and may grow up believing that it's acceptable or even expected to deny who they are. Once these children learn that they should conceal who they are, they may have to do a great deal of un-learning later in life to reclaim their wholeness. Also, children may learn to see giftedness itself as something wrong, or to be hidden. Being bright and having the ability to learn quickly can become something they are ashamed of, because it's hard for them to be proud of themselves for possessing these traits when their parents hide them.

## What It Looks Like

When talking with parents who deny their own giftedness, the refrain you will most often hear is, "I'm just a normal guy," or maybe, "I'm smart, but I'm not *gifted*." Despite having a lifetime of accolades and accomplishments, in spite of having quick minds and quick wit, they downplay their abilities and insist on describing themselves as "normal."

When it is suggested that their children's abilities may have been inherited from them, parents in denial frequently ascribe their children's gifts to the other parent, or they may even suggest that their children's abilities appeared out of nowhere. They will say things like, "She got it from her dad," or, "He sure didn't get that from me!"

Some parents who deny their own giftedness will assure you that their behavior is and always has been completely typical. This is especially true for parents who have grown up surrounded by gifted family and friends and who see their behavior as nothing out of the ordinary. When speaking with these parents, even when speaking of sometimes remarkable feats, you will often hear them ask some variation of, "Don't all kids do that?"

## EFT to Help

Many parents who read this book are willing to do just about anything to help their children. They'll learn about the experience of giftedness and how it affects their children's lives; they'll learn about this crazy-sounding tool called EFT, and even teach their children to tap on their foreheads as a means of emotional regulation. But many parents will draw the line at tapping on even the *possibility* that they may themselves be gifted. Their denial is so strong that they can't allow themselves to consider revising how they see themselves, even if it would help their children.

The script below, therefore, centers on resistance rather than on giftedness, per se. If you are a parent who is raising a gifted child and yet who considers yourself to not be gifted, I encourage you to tap through it. Obviously, I don't know you personally, so I can't say for sure whether you're gifted or not… but I encourage you to try this script anyway.

*Parental Denial*

As always, the script is here simply to get you started in your tapping. Use whatever words land for you and continue to tap at any point if it helps to clear any emotions which surface. You may also wish to keep pen and paper nearby to make note of any memories that may come up as you tap, so you can go back and clear them using the technique for clearing old memories described in Chapter Three.

| Point | Statement |
| --- | --- |
| *Karate chop* | Even though I'm quite sure I'm not gifted, I love and accept myself just as I am.<br><br>Even though I know I'm just an ordinary person raising a wonderful, gifted child, I love and accept myself fully.<br><br>Even though I may be smart, I'm not gifted and I'm fine with that, and I deeply and completely love, accept, and forgive myself exactly as I am. |
| *Above the eye* | I'm not gifted, |
| *Side of the eye* | And I'm okay with that. |
| *Under the eye* | I don't have to be gifted. |
| *Under the nose* | My {child is/ children are} gifted. |
| *Under the mouth* | But I don't have to be gifted to raise a gifted child. |
| *Collarbone* | I'm fine just the way I am. |

| Point | Statement |
|---|---|
| Under the arm | I don't need to give myself a new label at this point in my life. |
| Top of the head | I don't need to change how I see myself. |
| Above the eye | I don't need to think of myself differently from how I always have. |
| Side of the eye | And I have always known that I'm not gifted {because...} |
| Under the eye | And that's fine. |
| Under the nose | It's okay for me to know that about myself. |
| Under the mouth | But what if I'm wrong? |
| Collarbone | I'm so confident I'm not gifted. |
| Under the arm | I'm so certain of it. |
| Top of the head | But what if I'm denying this... |
| Above the eye | And it's true? |
| Side of the eye | Would that be such a bad thing? |
| Under the eye | Why do I feel such a need to insist that I'm not gifted? |
| Under the nose | Maybe I feel it's not a safe thing to admit. |
| Under the mouth | Maybe I don't want to stand out. |
| Collarbone | Maybe I've always felt stupid, |
| Under the arm | Or at least no smarter than anyone else! |
| Top of the head | How could I possibly be gifted? |
| Above the eye | But what if I am? |
| Side of the eye | What does my insistence that I'm not one of "those gifted people" mean to my child? |

## Parental Denial

| Point | Statement |
|---|---|
| *Under the eye* | What am I teaching my kid about giftedness, when I act like it can't possibly be true of me? |
| *Under the nose* | And maybe it's not true. Maybe I'm really not gifted. |
| *Under the mouth* | But my kid is pretty sharp. |
| *Collarbone* | {He/ she} sees that I'm pretty determined not to call myself gifted. |
| *Under the arm* | I wonder if this makes {him/ her} feel weird about the fact that {he/ she} is gifted? |
| *Top of the head* | Is it possible I make {him/ her} feel bad about being different from me? |
| *Above the eye* | Is it possible I make {him/ her} feel bad about being different from {his/her} classmates? |
| *Side of the eye* | I wonder what would happen if I opened myself to the possibility of being gifted? |
| *Under the eye* | I don't have to buy into the idea, |
| *Under the nose* | But maybe I shouldn't be quite so opposed to it anymore. |
| *Under the mouth* | Maybe I can open myself up to a new way of seeing myself. |
| *Collarbone* | Maybe I can choose to see myself as safe, no matter who I am or how I describe myself. |
| *Under the arm* | Maybe I can consider the possibility that fitting in shouldn't be more important than celebrating who I am – and who my kid is. |

*Tapping for the Gifted Child*

| Point | Statement |
|---|---|
| Top of the head | Maybe I can be open to the idea that the way I've always seen myself may be incomplete. |
| Above the eye | It may be true that I've always felt stupid, or at least not smart. |
| Side of the eye | But maybe there's more to the story than I've known. |
| Under the eye | Maybe it's time to open myself to new options. |
| Under the nose | I'm choosing now to open myself to seeing things differently. |
| Under the mouth | I know it's safe for me to see things differently. |
| Collarbone | I know it's possible for me to see things differently. |
| Under the arm | I know I'm worthy of seeing myself in the best possible light. |
| Top of the head | And I am willing to see my abilities, gifted or not, in the best possible way. |
| Above the eye | I'm willing to celebrate my gifts. |
| Side of the eye | Just as I'm willing to celebrate my child's gifts. |
| Under the eye | I'm willing to give up my denial. |
| Under the nose | I'm willing to give up my resistance to seeing myself through new eyes. |
| Under the mouth | Whether or not I'm gifted, I'm open to learning new things about myself. |
| Collarbone | And I choose to love even parts of myself I may not have recognized before. |

| Point | Statement |
|---|---|
| *Under the arm* | No matter what happened when I was younger, |
| *Top of the head* | It's okay to see myself today in new and healthy ways. |

*Take a deep breath in through your nose...*

*Hold it for a few seconds...*

*Release it slowly through your mouth.*

CHAPTER THIRTEEN

# Parental Triggering

George was shaking and literally seeing red. He could not *believe* he had just gotten a call asking him to pick up his son early from summer camp.

The camp was specifically for gifted children, and Jean-Luc was most certainly gifted, working a few years ahead of kids his own age in math and intense in everything he did. He was also a master negotiator who wouldn't break the letter of the law, but he would argue everything, looking for any loophole that would give him a few more minutes of screen time, an extra dessert, or a later bedtime. If anyone was supposed to understand him and his idiosyncrasies, it was expected to be a camp for gifted kids. But the camp director had just called, asking his dad to bring him home early. Jean-Luc's inability to follow the rules without arguing had pushed the counselors too far, and he was asked to leave due to his repeated disrespect of the staff.

George was beside himself with rage, and during the drive to camp, he kept thinking, "Jean-Luc isn't a bad kid! He just has a natural tendency to poke at people, trying to find the boundaries. Jeez, this camp director sounds exactly like my high school physics teacher, Mrs. Harrison – she could never handle my tendency to question things, either! Why are people so narrow minded all the time?!"

Although we discussed triggering extensively in Chapter Three, it is common, and important, enough that it's worth another look from the parental perspective.

As you recall, psychological triggering is the experience of having something in your immediate environment call to mind a previous, traumatic event, and then you respond as if you were going through the previous event rather than the current one. Triggering can contribute to all sorts of negative experiences for gifted kids, ranging from children suddenly losing it in the face of ongoing boredom, to the implosion that parents may see when their young perfectionists don't measure up to their own standards. But triggering also affects *parents* of gifted children, sometimes profoundly.

Many adults who are parenting gifted children were themselves gifted children once upon a time, and many of them suffered the ill effects of being misunderstood by a neurotypical world. They may have experienced boredom, bullying, isolation, depression, and misunderstanding when they were young, and in many cases, those wounds have not fully healed. We're told, "Time heals all wounds," but this simply isn't true. Far too many gifted adults are still carrying old hurts from their childhoods, and these sensitive memories may be triggered by their children's experiences.

It's common for parents of gifted children to experience at least occasional triggering of their own unresolved issues as their kids grow because the experiences of gifted children are often similar across generations, sometimes eerily so. For many years, gifted kids have expressed frustration with the slow pace of their classes, or have found themselves without anyone whom they consider a close friend. Because the gifted experience generally hasn't changed much since they were children, parents find that their children often experience incidents that resemble events in their own lives, subconsciously reminding the parents of their painful old memories. It could be any aspect of giftedness, from being bored in class to feeling like a fraud, but the parallels are often too pronounced for parents to escape untriggered.

When parents are triggered by their children's experiences, they may be unconsciously transported back to a time when they went through something similar – or at least to a time which seems to their amygdalas to be similar. In point of fact, the specific details between the child's situation and the parent's past may vary significantly, but the similarity in emotional tone will often trigger the parent's old issues. For example, if a daughter is not invited to a classmate's birthday party, it may, on some level, remind her father of the time he wasn't selected for the school play, triggering his old feelings of isolation. Although the specific incidents may differ a great

## Parental Triggering

deal, the parent may perceive that his child is being subjected to the same painful treatment he felt he received when young, and he may be triggered as a result.

In addition, parents who possess the common gifted trait of being passionate about justice may frequently find themselves being triggered by what they see as unfairness in their children's lives. In particular, rules and guidelines are often developed in schools and community groups based on neurotypical development patterns, and those rules may be enforced regardless of the abilities of the individual child in question. In some cases, younger gifted children may be capable of engaging in certain activities quite successfully, but they are prevented from doing so by age restrictions. In other cases, gifted children with learning or developmental disabilities may be expected to adhere to behavioral or other performance standards that don't take their limitations into account. In instances like these, justice-oriented parents may find their indignation over issues of fairness may be triggered, and anger and even outrage may surface.

Another situation in which parents may find themselves being triggered stems from being out of sync with the general population on the subject of giftedness itself. Once parents understand what giftedness truly means for gifted people, they may find themselves frustrated by the lack of understanding on the part of the people around them. They may become irritated by the fact that friends and neighbors just don't get why giftedness presents unique challenges, or they may grow tired of repeatedly having to explain to their children's

209

teachers and administrators the ways giftedness *really* affects their kids. As gifted adults, these parents are quick learners, and may have limited patience with others who learn more slowly. As Michele Kane describes it, "It can be like having to read *Good Night, Moon*, over and over." (Kane, 2016) While this common bedtime story may be a lovely book, it can be challenging for gifted adults to retain their enthusiasm for covering the same, simple material day after day, and situations like having to explain giftedness to yet another school administrator can trigger a parent's old pain and frustration over having experienced boredom when young, especially if they were forced to wait for slower learners to catch up in school.

As noted in Chapter Three, whenever someone has been triggered, he or she is responding to the previous event which has been called to mind, rather than the current one which acted as the triggering agent. In cases when parents have been triggered by something in their child's environment, the parent reacts to the historical event from his or her own past, rather than the situation facing his or her child today, which can sometimes cause parents to respond in inappropriate ways.

Also, when parents are responding based on their own pain, they are frequently unable to problem solve effectively, to put things into perspective, or to engage in empathetic reflection of their children's experiences and emotions, all of which cause children to suffer further. When children are encountering difficult circumstances, they are best served by adults who can model healthy emotional regulation and proactive problem-solving skills.

Adults who are feeling, and possibly even behaving, like wounded children, are rarely able to teach their children the necessary skills to address whatever problem has arisen.

## What It Looks Like

As noted previously, people rarely recognize that they, themselves, have been triggered. The most common things noticed by the people around them are that they may respond out of proportion to the current circumstance, or they may respond to things that don't appear to others to even have happened.

It's not uncommon for triggered parents to overreact to their children's problems. For instance, some parents whose children complain of feeling excluded may respond vehemently, demanding meetings with teachers and principals, hijacking parent-association meetings, or otherwise clamoring for inclusion and understanding on the parts of everyone at the school. Their reactions may be out of proportion to the actual incident; however, if they used to feel isolated when they were young, their response may be based on how they felt as children rather than the current situation.

Triggered parents may also seem to get carried away in tangential directions. For example, when children report feeling sad that they weren't invited to join some activity with classmates, their parents may respond by spearheading a massive anti-bullying campaign, even if the incident didn't involve bullying. The parents may be responding to some incident in their own pasts, rather than to the situation facing their children today.

Sometimes, triggered parents may identify so strongly with their suffering children that they feel that they, personally, are under attack, especially in the event of an egregious incident such as removal from an activity or overt conflict with another child. They behave as if they, rather than their children, are the ones facing the situation, or they may perceive an incident as an assault against the entire family. When speaking to school or community leaders, they may ask questions like, "How could you let this happen to us?" rather than, "How could this happen to my child?" In these circumstances, it may be almost impossible for parents to remember that whatever has happened isn't about them, but is about their kids, and it may be hard for them to constructively address the situation as a result.

## EFT to Help

If you believe that you or another gifted parent you know are being triggered by your children's experiences, I encourage you to go back and reread Chapter Three. The old emotions that surface when you're triggered may make it hard for you to think clearly until the episode has passed, but you have tools now to help deal with triggering when it arises. You can use the scripts in that chapter to limit the duration and intensity of the episode in the short term, and to remove the emotional charge from painful, triggered memories in the long term.

*Parental Triggering*

In this chapter, I want to offer you a very different script. I want to address your potential resistance to working on your own triggering issues, not because your kids need you to be at your best to help them – although they do – but because you deserve to heal. If you've been carrying around pain from your own gifted childhood and you're now a parent, teacher, or even a grandparent, that's far too long. You don't have to hurt anymore. It's okay for you to put those memories to rest so they won't be triggered again. Chapter Three will help you to do that, but here I want to try to make it so you'll actually turn back to Chapter Three and do that work, so please tap along.

As you well know by now, the script is here simply to help you get started. Feel free to change the words to ones that resonate with you, even using four-letter words if those are what land for you. Also, continue to tap at any point if it helps to clear any emotions which surface. You may also wish to keep paper and pencil handy to make note of any memories that may come up, so you can go back and clear them later.

| Point | Statement |
|---|---|
| *Karate chop* | Even though I don't want to deal with my triggering issues, I'm trying to love and accept myself anyway. |
| | Even though I'm not even sure I HAVE triggering issues, much less that I should address them, I accept myself and how I feel right now. |

*Tapping for the Gifted Child*

| Point | Statement |
|---|---|
|  | Even though I don't want to deal with any of this triggering stuff, I'm choosing to love and accept myself fully and completely. |
| *Above the eye* | I'm not really sure I have triggering issues. |
| *Side of the eye* | And I'm certainly not sure I need to deal with them. |
| *Under the eye* | I've gotten this far, |
| *Under the nose* | And while I'm not perfect, I get along. |
| *Under the mouth* | I take care of my kids. |
| *Collarbone* | I deal with things as they come up. |
| *Under the arm* | Who is this woman who doesn't even know me, that she thinks I should deal with my "triggering issues"?! |
| *Top of the head* | I'm fine the way I am. |
| *Above the eye* | It's not that I have lots of work to do on myself. |
| *Side of the eye* | I mean, who doesn't have some painful old memories from when they were a kid? |
| *Under the eye* | Everyone remembers times when the other kids were mean to them, |
| *Under the nose* | Or when they felt left out, or bored, or like a fraud at school. |
| *Under the mouth* | There's a reason most kids don't like going to school! |
| *Collarbone* | And yes, maybe I felt {bored/ lonely/ sad, etc} when I was a kid. |

## Parental Triggering

| Point | Statement |
|---|---|
| Under the arm | Maybe I {didn't have many friends/ felt stupid/ felt depressed, etc} when I was young. |
| Top of the head | But I'm fine now, and no author who doesn't even know me is going to tell me otherwise! |
| Above the eye | I don't have to do this tapping stuff for myself. |
| Side of the eye | I read this book for my {child/ grandchildren/ students, etc}, not for me! |
| Under the eye | No one can make me do this. |
| Under the nose | And I can carry those painful memories for my whole life if I want to! |
| Under the mouth | But if I'm honest, I don't actually want to. |
| Collarbone | I don't like hurting when I remember my childhood. |
| Under the arm | And I'm not convinced that this EFT thing is going to make it so my painful childhood memories are suddenly FINE, |
| Top of the head | But it can't hurt anything for me to try. |
| Above the eye | What if it were to work? |
| Side of the eye | What if I were to think back on those awful moments when I was a kid, and they didn't bother me anymore? |
| Under the eye | Wouldn't that be wonderful? |
| Under the nose | I'm not sure that would be wonderful, actually. |
| Under the mouth | It would be weird. |

*Tapping for the Gifted Child*

| Point | Statement |
|---|---|
| *Collarbone* | I'm so used to carrying these old hurts around, I'm not sure what it would be like to put them down. |
| *Under the arm* | But maybe it's time I found out. |
| *Top of the head* | Maybe it's time I allow myself to heal, at last. |
| *Above the eye* | So I'm choosing now to give this a try. |
| *Side of the eye* | I'm allowing myself to heal. |
| *Under the eye* | I choose to know I'm able to heal. |
| *Under the nose* | I choose to admit that I'm willing to heal. |
| *Under the mouth* | I choose to know I'm worthy of healing. |
| *Collarbone* | And I give myself permission to release the pain of my old memories. |
| *Under the arm* | I understand I may have to work through them one by one, |
| *Top of the head* | But it's time for me to do that, because I deserve to set myself free. |
| *Take a deep breath in through your nose...* | |
| *Hold it for a few seconds...* | |
| *Release it slowly through your mouth.* | |

CHAPTER FOURTEEN

# Parental Acceptance and The Journey Forward

Cindy sat at a table with other parents, watching her son Colin on the other side of the room. He was playing an elaborate board game with a handful of other seven- and eight-year-old boys, talking and smiling, something she hadn't seen him do outside their home in far too long. She couldn't hear their conversation, but one of the fathers at her table had recently come back and related that the boys were talking about space exploration. "I think they may have been designing an artificially intelligent Mars rover," the dad had reported with a laugh.

Colin's sudden laughter caught Cindy unaware. She couldn't quite believe this was the same child she had dragged to this afternoon gathering. Colin's persistent boredom in school had ultimately led to testing which indicated that he was exceptionally gifted, and Cindy had been in rather a panic ever since. How was she supposed to raise an exceptionally gifted child? Online searches had ultimately revealed a gifted support group that met in a museum not far from her home, and she had insisted that a very unwilling Colin come to a meeting. He had been utterly unconvinced that these children would differ in any way from the kids he saw daily, and he had only agreed to leave the car when his mom promised that he need not stay for more than 30 minutes.

To her shock, he was still happily engaged with kids his own age hours later. It seemed that being with children like himself let Colin relax, giving her time to ask endless questions of her fellow parents. "How did they deal with feelings of isolation in their own children? Could anyone recommend activities to appeal to his math-loving brain? What was the best way to talk to the school principal when Colin's needs weren't being met?"

The parents to whom she talked had answered question after question, but what Cindy most valued about the day was just watching these families. The parents were just parents, answering questions, assisting their children, and correcting them when necessary. The children were just children, asking endless questions, playing with other children, and arguing with their siblings. No one stared or pointed fingers when one of the children did something extraordinary. No one seemed to have giftedness-induced post-traumatic stress disorder. They were just families. If one didn't hear the topics of conversation, one would never know these families were anything out of the ordinary.

*"It is possible,"* Cindy found herself thinking. *"It's possible to raise a gifted child and not have endless scars to show for it. Maybe I can do this. Maybe we're going to be okay."*

*Parental Acceptance and
The Journey Forward*

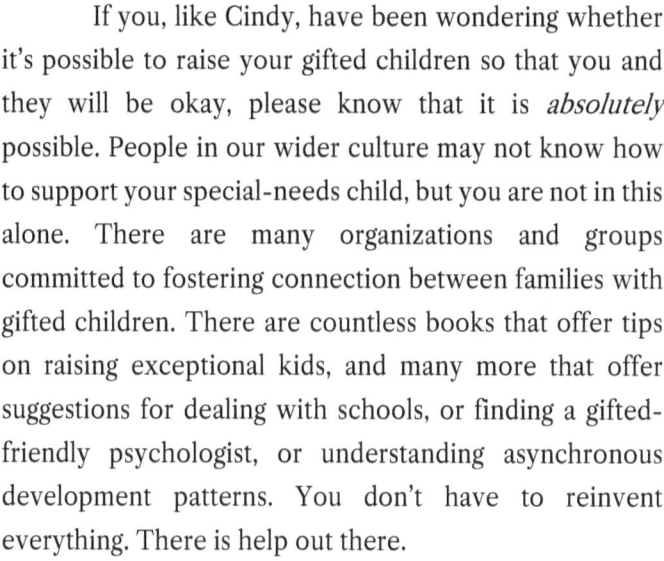

If you, like Cindy, have been wondering whether it's possible to raise your gifted children so that you and they will be okay, please know that it is *absolutely* possible. People in our wider culture may not know how to support your special-needs child, but you are not in this alone. There are many organizations and groups committed to fostering connection between families with gifted children. There are countless books that offer tips on raising exceptional kids, and many more that offer suggestions for dealing with schools, or finding a gifted-friendly psychologist, or understanding asynchronous development patterns. You don't have to reinvent everything. There is help out there.

The best advice I can offer right now is to simply calm down. If you've found your way to this book, odds are very good that your family is suffering in some way due to the giftedness in your home. That pain may make it difficult for you to see possible solutions to your family's problems, and your fear for your children's futures may make it difficult to remain optimistic about all the ways you can help your children succeed. But it's possible for gifted families to not only succeed but to thrive, and yours can be among them. Raising gifted children may not be easy, but it is thrilling to watch these young people develop into fascinating, multi-talented adults, and you can do it.

*Tapping for the Gifted Child*

I'm not including a tapping script in this chapter, because you already have the tools you need. Take a deep breath, tap away your own fear and anxiety, and then dive in to whatever challenges your children face. (Turn back to Chapter Ten if you need help dealing with your anxiety.) Remember, EFT can be applied to pretty much any pain, fear, or failure your children experience, so use it to reduce your children's suffering day by day. Tapping with your kids will help them feel heard, acknowledged, understood, and validated, and hopefully, you'll be able to guide them to release the pains and fears that might otherwise cause them lasting pain.

Regular tapping will allow your kids to move forward without carrying negative emotions or conclusions about themselves for having been different from other children, and their success will make it possible for you to be kinder to yourself as a parent. When you have the tools to help your children, and you can see that your efforts are making a difference, tapping will bring peace to you as surely as it does to your kids.

Ultimately, releasing negative emotions and conclusions about your family's gifted experiences will enable you and your children to embrace and enjoy your family's gifted journey. My hope is that the Emotional Freedom Techniques will help you to accept and welcome whatever amazing path your family takes through the gifted world.

APPENDIX I

# Resources

## For the Emotional Freedom Techniques

- [https://emofree.com/english/eft-tapping-tutorial-en.html](https://emofree.com/english/eft-tapping-tutorial-en.html) Gary Craig developed EFT, and his Gold Standard Tutorial is a great place to learn the ins and outs of performing it.

- [https://tappingqanda.com/](https://tappingqanda.com/) This resource-rich site covers EFT basics and provides hundreds of tap-along scripts you can use, but I think its greatest value lies in its ability to help you find new ways to incorporate the power of EFT into your life, such as tapping to improve decision-making, creativity, or gratitude.

- Remember, you can always go to YouTube and search for "EFT tapping," plus any problem you can think of. Many practitioners have posted tap-along videos for virtually every issue imaginable, making it possible to get the benefits of EFT without having to create your own scripts.

- For those of you who prefer books to websites, you may wish to look into the books by various members of the Ortner family, particularly *The Tapping Solution*, which talks generally about the power of EFT and how to perform it.

## For Giftedness

There are many resources that speak to raising gifted children; I'm including a few that I found most helpful.

- www.hoagiesgifted.org Created and curated by the mother of gifted children, Hoagies Gifted Education Page offers endless resources and reassurance to families on the gifted journey. From explaining common acronyms to suggesting great toys for wicked-smart kids, this site provides a wealth of information.

- http://giftedissues.davidsongifted.org/BB/ Although I am personally not a fan of the bulletin board format, there is lots of great parent-to-parent advice and information shared on this site, which is affiliated with the Davidson Institute for Talent Development.

- *Raising Your Spirited Child* by Mary Sheedy Kurcinka, although not explicitly written about gifted children, was the first book I encountered that helped me to deal with what I would now describe as gifted intensity. I very much appreciated her gentle approach.

- *High IQ Kids*, edited by Kiesa Kay, Deborah Robson, and Judy Fort Brenneman, offers a rare look into the world of exceptionally and profoundly gifted families. If your child is highly gifted, this book may offer much-needed reassurance.

- *The Mislabeled Child* by Brock and Fernette Eide was written for parents of children with notable learning differences. It includes a chapter on giftedness, but I think its real value is for parents of 2E kids, as it offers reassurance and strategies to support children with a wide variety of diagnoses.

*Resources*

- *Off the Charts: Asynchrony and the Gifted Child*, edited by Christine Neville, Michael Piechowski, and Stephanie Tolan, offers a comprehensive look at how asynchronous development affects all areas of a gifted individual's life. It includes chapters such as, "Life in the Asynchronous Family," and "Giftedness Across the Lifespan." It is a rather academic book, but it offers helpful reminders that no matter what gifted issue your family is facing, you're not alone.

- I remain convinced that nothing is as valuable to parents raising gifted children as time spent with other parents who are raising similar children, and nothing is as valuable to gifted children as time spent with other gifted children. If your family is gifted, I encourage you to find a way to meet with other gifted families in real life. There are organizations in virtually every state that can connect you to others; here are a few US-based national organizations you may wish to investigate:
    - The National Association for Gifted Children (NAGC) https://www.nagc.org/
    - Serving the Emotional Needs of the Gifted (SENG) https://www.sengifted.org/
    - Johns Hopkins Center for Talented Youth (CTY) https://cty.jhu.edu/
    - Duke University Talent Identification Program (Duke TIP) https://tip.duke.edu/
    - Davidson Institute for Talent Development http://www.davidsongifted.org/
    - PG Retreat https://pgretreat.org/

# Acknowledgements

I work in the very narrow niche where the EFT and gifted worlds intersect. Over the years, I have been fortunate to learn from many people in each of these areas, and while there are more people than I could possibly name, I'd like to thank a few of them at this time.

I'd like to thank classmate Diane Dhao for asking, "What is your book going to be about?" Her offhand question set me on a path I had never thought to follow.

I am grateful to Gary Craig for making EFT freely available to the world, and I want to thank those whose knowledge of EFT has, with or without their awareness, helped me to heal and grow in ways I could never have anticipated: Jennifer Duff, Brad Yates, Deborah Lindsey, Chantal Quesnal, Claudia Braun, Andrew Lukonis, and Gene Monterastelli.

In the gifted world, I have been particularly fortunate to learn from Michele Kane, Linda Silverman, and Sue Jackson, among many others. I'm not permitted to "out" the families who welcomed us to the gifted world and taught us what it really meant to be gifted, but I hope the members of PG Retreat and the Davidson Young Scholars program know how very thankful we are to know them all.

## Acknowledgements

Thanks to Gina Mallonee for design brilliance and to Deb Porter for her utterly invaluable assistance as I developed my practice. I'd also like to thank Robin Herbison and Deb Nowak, who read and reread this book in part or in whole during writing.

Special thanks to Cass Sackett at Zero K Press for publishing this book, and for all the help and support that went into the process.

I particularly want to thank three people who have, over the years, believed in me, encouraged me, and loaned me their courage and strength when my own have faltered. Emily Hostetter, Michele Kane, and Ashok Sudarshan, I cannot thank you enough.

And to my family, without whom this would never have been possible: Justin Chamberlin, thanks for enabling me to do this work, and Claire Chamberlin, thanks for choosing me. I love you both.

# References

Akil, H. (2016). The Biology of Emotions. *Brain and Behavior Research Foundation Quarterly*, 6-8.

Church, D., Yount, G., & Brooks, A. J. (2012, October). The Effect of Emotional Freedom Techniques on Stress Biochemistry: A Randomized Controlled Trial. *The Journal of Nervous and Mental Disease*, pp. 891-896.

Cornwell, B. (2015, August 28). *Parabola*. Retrieved February 2016, from http://parabola.org/2015/08/28/gifts-for-gifted-children/

Gross, M. (2002, May 2). "Play Partner" or "Sure Shelter": What gifted children look for in friendship. *SENG Newsletter*.

Gross, M. (2006). Tips for Parents: Gifted Children's Friendships. *YS Parent Seminars*.

*I Need a Lighthouse*. (2015). Retrieved March 23, 2016, from Teen Depression: https://www.ineedalighthouse.org/depression-suicide/teen-depression/

Jackson, P. S., & Peterson, J. (2004). Depressive Disorder in Highly Gifted Adolescents. *The Journal of Secondary Gifted Education*, 175–186.

*References*

Kanazawa, S., & Perina, K. (2009, December 13). *Psychology Today*. Retrieved December 2015, from The Scientific Fundamentalist: https://www.psychologytoday.com/blog/the-scientific-fundamentalist/200912/why-do-so-many-women-experience-the-imposter-syndrome

Kane, M. (2016, February). Professor, College of Education, Northeastern Illinois University. (W. Chamberlin, Interviewer)

Kottmeyer, C. (2008). *Hoagies Gifted Education Page*. Retrieved December 16, 2015, from http://www.hoagiesgifted.org/never_say_bored.htm

Lind, S. (2001). Overexcitability and the Gifted. *SENG Newsletter*, 3-6.

Malone, T. (2004, February 08). *Susan Ohanian.com*. Retrieved December 7, 2015, from http://susanohanian.org/show_special_news.php?id=269

*Merriam Webster.com*. (n.d.). Retrieved January 10, 2016, from http://www.merriam-webster.com/dictionary/perfectionism

Mowrer, O. (1965). Symptoms of Development. *Contemporary Psychology*, 538-540.

Natcharian, L. (2010, July 15). Retrieved January 2016, from http://blog.masslive.com/real_learning/2010/07/meet_the_perfectionists.html

*National Institutes of Health.* (2014). Retrieved March 24, 2016, from Major Depression Among Adolescents: http://www.nimh.nih.gov/health/statistics/prevalence/major-depression-among-adolescents.shtml

*National Institutes of Health.* (2015). Retrieved March 18, 2016, from Any Anxiety Disorder Among Adults: http://www.nimh.nih.gov/health/statistics/prevalence/any-anxiety-disorder-among-adults.shtml

Neihart, M. (1999). The Impact of Giftedness on Psychological Well-Being. *Roeper Review.* Retrieved from http://sengifted.org/archives/articles/the-impact-of-giftedness-on-psychological-well-being

Neihart, M., Reis, S. M., Robinson, N. M., & Moon, S. M. (2002). *The Social and Emotional Development of Gifted Children: What Do We Know?* Prufrock Press.

Ransom, D. (2014, April 23). *The Pinakes.* Retrieved February 17, 2016, from http://thepinakes.com/2014/04/quotes-on-the-internet-frederick-douglass-and-repairing-broken-men/

*Statistics Brain.* (2015, March 27). Retrieved March 22, 2016, from Teen Suicide Statistics: http://www.statisticbrain.com/teen-suicide-statistics/

Tillier, B. (1995, October 26). *The Theory of Positive Disintegration by Kasimierz Dabrowski.* Retrieved

*References*

March 23, 2016, from Overview: www.positivedisintegration.com

*World Health Organization*. (2015, October). Retrieved March 12, 2016, from Fact Sheet 369: http://www.who.int/mediacentre/factsheets/fs369/en/

# Index

Anxiety, 168–70
B vitamin deficiency, 173
Beliefs, 117–19, 138–40
Boredom, 66–68
Cognitive dissonance, 77
Dabrowski, Kazimierz, 182–85
Depression, 144–50
Emotional Freedom Techniques
   Clearing beliefs, 119
      Table top model, 120
   Clearing fear, 115, 175
   Clearing trauma, 22, 56, 57
   Flexibility, 22
   Movements, 27–31
   Personal Peace Procedure, 153
   Relieving physical pain, 157
      Chasing the Pain, 158
   Side effects, 41
   Words, 31–34
Energetic blocks, 24, 26
Gifted children, 11, 12
   Depression of, 145
   Levels of Giftedness, 16
Gifted traits
   Asynchrony, 13
   Empathy, 14, 18, 19
   Intensity, 13
   Justice, 14
   Overexcitabilities, 183–84
   Sensitivity, 14, 169
Imposter syndrome, 75–78, *169*
Isolation, 126–30, 169
Magnesium deficiency, 172
Overexcitabilities. *See* Gifted traits, Overexcitabilities
Perfectionism, 104–6, 169

*Index*

Personal Peace Procedure. *See* Emotional Freedom Techniques, Personal Peace Procedure
Resistance, 42
   Identity-based, 42
   Secondary Gain-based, 43

SUDs scale, 34
Theory of Positive Disintegration, 182–85
Triggering, 48–51, 73, 95, 110, 170, 175, 207
Twice exceptionality, 16, 88–91, 170

www.ingramcontent.com/pod-product-compliance
Lightning Source LLC
Chambersburg PA
CBHW020647300426
44112CB00007B/274